# ROMAN GARDENS
## and their
# PLANTS

Claire Ryley
Illustrations by Sally Rigby

**Acknowledgements**

The author gratefully acknowledges the assistance given by the Sussex Archaeological Society, and David Rudkin in particular for his support. She also thanks Dr Christopher Thacker for the loan of many of the Latin texts. Professor Marijke van der Veen generously sent a copy of her article published in 2008, updating information about plants introduced into Britain during the Roman period.

The author takes full responsibility for any errors that may have occurred in the text.

ISBN 0-904973-16-6

Printed by St Richard's Press, Leigh Road, Chichester, West Sussex PO19 8TU Tel: 01243 782988

# CONTENTS

# ROMAN GARDENS AND THEIR PLANTS

There has been considerable research into Roman gardens, much of it based on archaeological work. The emphasis in the past has focused mainly on overall design and large permanent features, such as terraces, fountains, statuary, walls and other structures. More recently however, with the advance of scientific techniques used by archaeo-botanists, many plants have been identified from Roman sites within the Roman Empire, including Britain.

In 1994 I was asked to produce a list of plants for a new Roman garden at Fishbourne Roman Palace in West Sussex, and I found that although information was available about the landscaping of Roman gardens, there was very little written about the plants themselves.

This book was an attempt to rectify that omission, and perhaps inspire its readers to plant their own Roman garden. Since it was first published, there have been many more discoveries, and in 2006 an exhibition at the Museum of Garden History brought together a list of all the plants known to have been introduced to Britain in the Roman period, or shortly before.

The first part of the book describes the development of gardens during the Romano-British period (AD 43–410), both in Britain and elsewhere in the Roman Empire. The second part lists a selection of commonly grown plants and their significance to the Romans.

# FINDING THE EVIDENCE

There are two main sources of information, the first being classical literature, and the second, archaeological evidence.

Several relevant and useful works by Greek and Roman writers have survived. The principal texts about plants are *De Plantis* by Theophrastus, written in about 300 BC; *De Materia Medica* by Dioscorides, a Greek soldier serving in the Roman army in the 1st century AD; and *Historia Naturalis* by Pliny the Elder (AD 23–79).

There are also treatises on farming by Varro (116–27 BC), Cato (234–149 BC) and Columella (1st century AD), and lyric poetry by Virgil (70–19 BC) and Horace (65–8 BC), all of which contribute to our knowledge of Roman gardens.

Roman writing about plants tends to be practical and is often written in the form of a manual, describing farming techniques, or the medicinal use of plants.

Taken together these texts certainly give us a wide range of plants, but there are several problems in using the information to recreate an authentic Roman garden. It is not always possible to identify a plant from the author's

*Detail of a rose garden from a fresco, Casa del Bracciale d'Oro Pompeii, first century AD.*

description. This may be because there are problems in translation, or simply that the writer did not describe the plant accurately, or in sufficient detail.

Some plants have changed due to cultivation or cross-fertilisation, so varieties described may no longer resemble their modern counterparts.

We cannot always establish whether plants were grown in gardens even when we are able to identify them and know that they were regarded as useful. For instance Dioscorides recorded about 600 plants used to treat patients for a wide variety of ailments. His book *De Materia Medica* is fascinating and sometimes rather gruesome, but does not usually specify whether the plants were cultivated in gardens or gathered from the wild.

Lastly, writers are in the main describing gardens and plants in Italy or other Mediterranean countries, so although their information may apply to Roman gardens in Britain, we cannot always assume this to be the case. Our colder climate alone will have meant that some plants would not have survived here, even if an optimistic Roman gardener had brought them here from sunnier climes.

Archaeological research into plants has developed dramatically in the last 30 years or so, particularly spurred on by the pioneering work of Wilhelmina Jashemski on the Roman gardens at Pompeii and several villas in the Campania region of Italy.

Excavations have helped us to establish the size and layouts of various types of garden. They have also given us clues about how the gardens were used, whether as spaces for working, relaxing or dining, or for providing food, flowers and medicinal herbs for the owners' use. Analysis of pollen, carbonised remains, and other plant material, has shown the presence of a wide variety of plants, while at Pompeii, cavities left by tree roots have helped determine which trees flourished there nearly 2000 years ago. Wilhelmina Jashemski also used aerial photographs taken from balloons to enable her to study soil contours, for the purpose of locating the outlines of beds and other features.

Unfortunately, environmental archaeology is unlikely to give us a complete picture, because some plant remains survive much better than others, and particular soil conditions may mean that very little is found. For example, at Fishbourne Roman Palace archaeologists have discovered the probable site of the kitchen garden, not from plant remains, but from dark soil containing heavily abraded pottery fragments. The dark soil indicates that manure was added to the original soil, and the condition of the pottery suggests that the soil was frequently turned, for gardening purposes.

Another difficulty is that we cannot easily tell whether the plants identified were regarded as weeds or as useful to the Roman gardener. For example, fat hen (*Chenopodium album*) is now unwelcome in most vegetable gardens, but was a widely used potherb in Roman and other periods.

Roman mosaics and wall paintings form another valuable source of archaeological evidence and are our only pictorial descriptions of gardens and plants. In some, plants can be clearly identified, while others generate heated debate.

Despite these problems in interpretation of sources, and the partial nature of the evidence, it is possible to identify many important features of Roman gardens and an expanding list of plants commonly found in them.

## GARDENS OF THE WESTERN ROMAN EMPIRE

Although a garden (*hortus*) had long been an essential requirement for any household, Roman garden design was utilitarian until the 1st century BC, plants being grown for their usefulness rather than their beauty. They were sown in mixed informal beds in a cottage garden style, and were used for food, medicine and for religious purposes. The most commonly grown plants included cabbages, onions, peas, lettuces and root vegetables. Flowers such as violets and roses were cultivated for use as offerings on the shrines of household gods. Gradually other flowers were added, such as lilies and poppies, partly for their religious, but also for their decorative value. Rather than for beautifying the garden itself however, they were used to make garlands and wreaths for decorating the house or its occupants. Indeed, such was the demand for roses and violets, that they were grown on a large scale commercially around Rome and Naples in the 1st century AD. Flowers were also used in the perfume industry, and roses, lilies, mallows and violas have been identified in the garden of a Roman perfume factory at Pompeii.

Excavations at Pompeii by Wilhelmina Jashemski have shown that a wide variety of gardens existed in towns in the 1st century AD and before. Some lay in open ground at the edges of the town, but most were internal courtyard gardens. These could only be

*A bust of Spring with roses.*
Photographer: Gilles Mermet

reached by passing through a front door and entrance hall (*atrium*) that separated them from the street. Even the smallest garden must have given its users welcome relief from the dust and noise of the city. Many of the poorer townhouses had very small courtyards or simply a light well. These appear to have contained the mixed utilitarian planting of the earlier rural gardens, or one or two pots, perhaps for herbs or a few flowers.

In most houses the atrium was an open-air room, with a large rectangular hole (*compluvium*) in the centre of the roof. The rain which fell into the unroofed area was collected in a pool (*impluvium*) in the centre of the *atrium*. An overflow channel in the wall of the *impluvium* allowed excess water to flow into an underground cistern, which could be reached by a small wellhead set beside the *impluvium*. The potential for raising plants in the *atrium* was not wasted, and some *impluvia* have been found with circular or square planters built around them.

Large houses in the growing towns were built with rooms arranged around open courtyards (*peristylia*) at the rear of the properties, and it was in these that the first formal pleasure gardens were designed and planted. As the courtyards were regarded as outdoor rooms, seating, dining areas (*triclinia*), sundials, statues and wall-paintings feature in many of those found at Pompeii and other Roman urban sites. Evidence, such as food remains, loom weights and personal items, shows that their owners spent much of their time in their gardens, whether working, eating or relaxing.

In many instances a colonnade ran around one or more sides of the garden to offer a covered walkway. Fence panels were often inserted in the spaces between columns, the end posts being cut into the stone of the columns themselves. Some colonnades even had curtains which could be drawn to protect the walkway from rain or fierce sun. The walls of many colonnades were painted with garden scenes, and it is from these that we can identify many of the plants which are likely to have grown in the garden itself. The painters depict fencing, walls and flowing fountains in many of these paintings, as well as birds and insects, so we can visualise the ideal Roman garden even if the paintings were not matched by reality.

With the introduction of aqueducts in the Augustan period (27 BC–AD 14), pools and fountains became common, further enhancing the attractiveness of gardens. Square postholes indicate that pergolas were

*A garden shrine, Pompeii.*

*Millet and grapevines in a Tunisian mosaic.*
*Photographer: Gilles Mermet*

constructed in several gardens, and that climbing plants, such as vines, were trained over them. Sometimes a pergola was built over the *triclinium* or over a pool in the centre of the garden to offer shade from the summer sun. Romans often kept pet fish in pools, so it was important to protect them. Although the Romans did not use many climbing plants, ivy, vines, honeysuckle or clematis may have been used.

The plants grown in formal gardens were mainly evergreens such as box, rosemary, ivy, bay and myrtle. These were selected because they provided all year foliage, and needed little watering. They could also be clipped and trained according to the owner's whim, to provide often fantastic figures and even complex scenes, such as hunts or naval battles.

A few varieties of flowering plants, roses, stocks (*violarii*), Madonna lilies, oleanders and acanthus among them, were grown in courtyard gardens. Raised beds were recommended so that the plants could be seen from inside the house.

Some of the plants grown were associated with Roman gods, so it is not surprising that shrines are found in gardens, and that religious ceremonies took place in them. Of particular importance were Diana, goddess of the groves; Venus who watched over gardens; and Mars, god of all growing things.

Other types of garden found in Pompeii should be mentioned here. For those who had no gardens at all, there were well-planted public parks with huge plane trees providing shade. Market gardens and orchards provided town-dwellers with food and flowers, and vineyards produced wine on a large commercial scale. The Romans were nothing if not practical, and some gardens incorporated dining areas and latrines in their design. One latrine built into the corner of a peristyle appears to have had a large fig tree growing next to it, partly for privacy and partly to provide a handy supply of leaves for personal use! Other gardens were found around temples, and there are several examples of garden restaurants with permanent outdoor seating.

From the middle of the 1st century BC onwards, the range and varieties of plants available widened considerably, as introductions were made from newly conquered territories. For instance, Lucullus, a high ranking military official, is believed to have brought back apricots, peaches and cherries, after serving in the Asia in the 1st century BC. A hundred years later Emperor Vitellius introduced pistachio nuts to Italy from Syria. A comparison between the lists of some of the varieties of fruit trees known to Cato (2nd century BC) and Pliny (1st century AD) illustrates the increased range available.

|        | Pears | Apples | Figs | Plums | Quince |
|--------|-------|--------|------|-------|--------|
| **Cato**  | 5     | 4      | 6    | -     | -      |
| **Pliny** | 39    | 23     | 29   | 9     | 4      |

[Taken from *Roman Farming* by K D White]

There is strong evidence that such fruit trees as figs, apricots and plums were trained along walls or used as screens, while plane trees were frequently planted to give shade in the heat of summer. Wall-painters depict arbutus, cherry trees, lemon and citron trees, pomegranates, quinces and viburnums. In one garden at Pompeii, at the House of Polybius, tree roots indicate that in a garden approximately 9m², there were two fig trees, two cherry or pear trees and an olive tree, all of which would have provided shade as well as fruit.

Amazingly, the outline of the fruit-picker's ladder, some 8m. long, was found lying diagonally across the garden. Other unusual finds in the same garden were broken pieces of pots with four circular holes around their bases. Pliny describes such planting pots being used for transporting citron trees. In an excavation at Torre Annunziata near Naples, Wilhelmina Jashemski discovered a peristyle garden with four-holed planting pots buried in pairs near the pillar bases. She writes that the pots nearest the columns probably contained climbing plants, as the pots were buried

*A plant pot found at Fishbourne Roman Palace.*

at an angle towards the pillars. The pots in the second set were upright so they possibly contained evergreen shrubs or small trees, such as lemon trees.

As the Roman Empire prospered throughout the 1st century AD, a wealthier and more leisured class of citizens emerged. The upwardly mobile removed themselves for part of the year from the increasingly crowded and noisy towns to villas in the country. These ranged from commercially run farming and industrial economic units (*villae rusticae*) to luxurious rural retreats (*villae urbanae*). The former were built around courtyards, with accommodation for people, animals, carts and tools, and various farming activities such as wine-pressing or olive-crushing. The owner might also have a small courtyard garden for flowers and herbs.

Luxury villas were a very different matter. There commercial considerations

*A great estate shown in a floor mosaic from Tunisia.*
*Photographer: Gilles Mermet*

were of secondary importance. The inward orientation of the town garden was reversed in the country, and rural or sea views became an important part of garden design. Some of these private gardens were built on an enormous and lavish scale. A garden discovered at Herculaneum attached to the Villa of the Papyri had a peristyle which measured 100m by 33m. A pool 66m long by 7m wide was installed in the centre, and water was supplied to it from a subterranean aqueduct by means of a hydraulic system. Many valuable bronze and marble statues surrounded the pool and it would be hard to imagine a more opulent display of wealth and sophisticated technology. This particular garden has been carefully reproduced at the J. Paul Getty Museum in California.

Pliny the Younger, nephew of Pliny the Elder, wrote a detailed and loving description of his villa at Laurentum, which was primarily for winter use. He described the garden which was clearly precious to him. A box hedge, with rosemary planted to fill the gaps where the box was slow to establish, was planted all around the drive. The inner ring of the hedge surrounded an ornamental vine pergola, and mulberries and figs abounded throughout the garden. A terrace was carefully placed to protect its users from extremes of temperature and strong winds, and was thoughtfully scented with violets.

*The garden of the J. Paul Getty Museum, California, USA. Based on one found at a villa in Herculaneum.*

Incidentally, the Roman term *viola* covers not only violets, but stocks and wallflowers too.

Pliny the Younger also describes another villa in Tuscany at the foot of the Apennines. The soil was rich and well watered, but as the climate proved too cold for myrtle and olive trees, Pliny contented himself with bays, cypresses, and fruit trees. The villa faced south and was fronted by a broad colonnade. The sunny terrace was laid out with box hedges clipped into the shapes of animals, and a lower terrace was filled with acanthus. A dining room overlooked a small courtyard shaded by four plane trees with a fountain playing in a marble basin in the centre, and elsewhere fountains splashed and watered the garden. Throughout his descriptions of these gardens Pliny describes surroundings designed to please all the senses. Comfort, lovely views, delightful scents and the sound of splashing water all contribute to this aim. Pliny also admires the views of the meadows and woods beyond his domain for their natural beauty in contrast with the manicured elegance of his gardens.

While Pliny describes the pleasures of his villa's garden in glowing terms, Columella gives a much more down-to-earth description of a well-tended and productive garden. He comments on the increasing popularity of gardening in contrast with the "half-hearted and negligent" attitude prevailing in the past, and gives advice to the amateur horticulturalist – the Roman equivalent of gardening magazines and books today. He wrote that gardens should be planted with flowers to give colour and variety for much of the year. Snowdrops, narcissi, antirrhinums, marigolds and gladioli should be planted for spring, followed by roses, violets, amaranthus, lotus flowers, pansies and celandines in summer.

Columella advises growing a mouth-watering variety of vegetables, including less well known ones such as cardoon, purslane, skirret and alexanders. He also gives recommendations for sowing herbs:

> *"Now is the time, if pickles cheap you seek,*
> *To plant the caper and harsh elecampane*
> *And threatening fennel; creeping roots of mint*
> *And fragrant flowers of dill are spaced now*
> *And rue, which the Palladian berry's taste*
> *Improves, and mustard which will make him weep*
> *Whoe'er provokes it..."*

Palladian berries are olives, and fennel is "threatening" because it was used for caning naughty schoolboys.

Fruit trees provided a harvest of apples, apricots, peaches, plums, damsons, figs, mulberries and pomegranates.

The successful gardener should have a surplus to sell, and Columella describes baskets of rushes and willow twigs piled high with fruits and flowers to be taken to town. He

*Gathering olives*
*Photographer: Gilles Mermet*

*A mosaic of the estate of Lord Julius in Tunisia.*
*Photographer: Gilles Mermet*

also mentions the carrier returning from market, his pockets full of cash, and obviously a little inebriated!

Larger gardens permitted their owners to include "optional extras". Varro writes that a variety of enclosures can be used "for profit and for pleasure". These included aviaries, fishponds, hare enclosures, snail runs, dormice enclosures and even deer parks. Bees were kept whenever possible, for honey and wax were both valuable commodities. Varro, Columella and Pliny all give advice about the construction of beehives, their positioning, and suitable plants to attract bees and improve the flavour of the honey. Thyme, clover and lemon balm are three of the most important bee-plants.

Remains of Roman gardens have survived elsewhere in the Roman Empire. Due to the hot dry conditions in North Africa, it has been possible to excavate some fine gardens in Tunisia. Although similar to those in Italy, there are one or two differences. The warmer climate allowed date palms to flourish and produce fruit, but the lack of water would have inhibited the growth particularly of annuals and flowering plants. Mosaics were laid outside as well as inside villas, to decorate paths, pools and seating areas.

In Portugal, near the modern city of Coimbra, the remains of Roman Conimbriga have been excavated to reveal magnificent houses and remarkable gardens. In some, self-contained island flower beds have been found in central pools. Flowers were watered with jets playing from the many fountains. The designs are strictly geometric, combining straight lines and right angles with semicircular curves. The arches of sparkling splashing water from the fountains add to the effect, which can still be enjoyed today. These

*The water garden at Conimbriga, Portugal.*

*A wall painting of a villa and its formal garden from the house of Luctretius Fronto, in Pompeii.*

garden features and the fine mosaics in the peristyle gardens as well as in the houses show us how wealthy the owners must have been.

Gardens have also been found in France and Germany. One garden near Cologne has a more random and rather charming design, reconstructed by archaeologists from botanical remains. The villa and gardens measure about 100m by 90m. Paths meander between buildings built around the perimeter of the villa, and the garden was dedicated to several uses: a vegetable plot, an orchard, a small oak wood, a pond shaded by three alder trees, and open grassy spaces. Three rubbish dumps were also discovered, strategically placed near the house or animal stalls. A thorn hedge surrounding the vegetable plot and the entire perimeter of the garden would have kept out stray animals or undesirable visitors. The garden is very practical, but seems to have evolved rather than to have been planned from the outset.

As can be seen, Roman gardens came in many shapes, sizes and styles. The development of formal pleasure gardens contrasted with the informal planting in many town and rural gardens. Even the poorest homes grew plants if possible and wall-paintings show a keen interest in the natural world. Moreover, the ability to tame and control the natural world was dear to a Roman's heart, because outside the "civilised" towns and surrounding farmland lay vast areas of wilderness where he was unable to impose order and authority.

Because of limited space, plants were selected with a particular function in mind. They had to earn their place in the garden, whether as shade-providers, food, medicine or as decorative material. Gardens were at the heart of the home in position and in practice, much as a farmhouse kitchen might be in our colder climate.

# ROMAN GARDENS IN BRITAIN

One grey, cold, drizzly day, several years ago, I visited a remote and desolate settlement in Tasmania – the penal colony at Port Arthur. The beautiful stark buildings, standing in a bare muddy valley, are memorials to harsh regimes and deprivation. In contrast, on a slight promontory stands the prison governor's house, surrounded by a lovely mature garden. There is an old walnut tree near the house, planted by the first governor. This, with other imported plants, was his attempt to create an English garden in an alien environment many miles from home.

In much the same way, nearly two thousand years earlier, some of the civilian and military officials posted to new Roman colonies may have planned and planted gardens based on those "back home". These provided familiar and fitting surroundings for Roman villas, and were suited to the lifestyle of affluent Romans, though probably not to the British climate.

Gardens in Britain before the Roman conquest appear to have been restricted to small herb and vegetable plots within a roundhouse enclosure, or to "sacred groves", clearings in woods where religious rites took place. Although Britain was renowned for its efficient and productive farming, the main crops were cereals, such as wheat, oats, barley and a few pulses. Fruit, nuts and some vegetables were gathered from the wild, and growing food in orchards and kitchen gardens does not seem to have been common practice.

Garden archaeologists Robert Scaife and Peter Murphy (4) write that in prehistoric times people divided plants into five categories: (a) domesticated crops; (b) encouraged weeds; (c) tolerated weeds; (d) discouraged weeds; and (e) noxious weeds. The distinction between cultivated and wild plants was not as important to Iron Age people as their usefulness or otherwise as food or medicine.

Four types of garden evolved during the period of Roman occupation based on those in Italy: the formal; the semi-formal; the "natural"; and the kitchen garden. Planting in these gardens included a mixture of native and introduced plants, and only one type, the kitchen garden, was entirely utilitarian.

*A model of Fishbourne Roman Palace and its formal gardens.*

The early villas in Britain were for the most part quite small, and usually formed part of working farms geared to crop production or small scale industrial use. Kitchen gardens and vegetable plots were essential features, especially in rural areas where self-sufficiency was the norm.

*Box hedging planted into Roman bedding trenches at Fishbourne Roman Palace.*

However, as the owners became wealthier, wings were added to villas, forming open courtyards. More formal and decorative gardens were positioned in these courtyards leading to the main part of the villa, and farming paraphernalia and animals were banished to less visible areas. For example, at Frocester Court, Gloucestershire, the road leading to the villa takes the visitor past five beds for plants, flanked to the east by a gravelled area and to the west perhaps by an orchard. It appears that the beds were enriched with compost as various personal items and pieces of pottery were mixed in the soil, which may have arrived there via the compost heap where kitchen rubbish was dumped. At a villa in Latimer, in Buckinghamshire, archaeologists found an area outside the central porch paved with rectangular limestone slabs, and a fishpond measuring 13m by 2.6m in the centre of the courtyard. Both these examples of villa gardens date to the 4th century AD, and we know that in the 3rd and especially the 4th century, many villas were extended and expensively improved, and the gardens were similarly expanded and upgraded.

Two exceptionally large 1st century Roman buildings with gardens have been excavated, both of which, because of their size and probable owners, have been designated "palaces". The first palace was found in West Sussex, at Fishbourne. Excavations in the 1960s revealed not only a huge palatial building, but also gardens on a scale and in a style previously unknown in Britain. Indeed, the palace is typical of Roman design in Italy, and its size and opulence allows it to be compared favourably with imperial palaces in Rome. Five types of garden existed in and around the rectangular palace, these being (a) a large formal garden; (b) five small peristyle gardens; (c) a semi-formal garden to the east of the Palace; (d) kitchen gardens; and (e) a "natural" garden to the south of the South Wing.

The central formal garden measured approximately 75m by 90m and is by far the largest found in Britain. It was bisected by a central path which led from the Entrance Hall to the Audience Chamber.

*Bedding trenches and water pipes excavated in Fishbourne Roman Palace garden.*

One of the most exciting discoveries was the presence of bedding trenches, visible as dark lines dug into the clay sub-soil, which clearly showed the complex geometric shapes of the hedging. The hedge may well have been planted with box, which has been replanted in the trenches. The peristyle gardens in the North and East Wings were accessible only from rooms and corridors, and not from the central garden. They would have afforded a high degree of privacy and must have been pleasant retreats on dry days and on warm summer evenings.

Unfortunately we do not know what was grown in them, but it is likely that they contained seating, perhaps a pool and some decorative or sweet-smelling plants. A kitchen garden was sited on the area lying on the outside of the palace at the junction of the North and the West Wings. This was conveniently near the ovens, and protected from salt-laden winds from the nearby sea, and would have been screened from the wealthy owner and his visitors within the palace walls. This garden probably even had its own water supply, as archaeologists found a wooden water pipe complete with iron connecting collars within its boundaries.

The fourth garden was an unexpected discovery, lying between the South Wing and the sea. The ground was artificially terraced and a length of water pipe and a pool were found. Irregular holes found in the terrace may have been made by tree roots. Professor Barry Cunliffe, who excavated the site from 1971 onwards, writes that it is tempting to think that Fishbourne's wealthy owner appreciated the sea view and had constructed a "natural" garden which would merge with the countryside on the other side of the inlet.

No positive identifications of plants in the southern garden have been made, but there is scope for further work as there is well preserved organic material below the water table in the deep water channel that forms its southern boundary. As Professor Cunliffe writes: "It is not too much to hope that the gardeners responsible for the upkeep of the Fishbourne gardens tipped their clippings and rubbish over the terrace edge into the water!"

Further excavations in 1983 and 1985–1986 found remains of another semi-formal garden to the east of the Palace, situated on the northern side of the approach road from Chichester (the Roman town of *Noviomagus*). Excavations in this area revealed bedding trenches and a planter pot of the type found by Wilhelmina Jashemski at Pompeii.

The second palatial garden found in Britain is now unfortunately buried beneath Cannon Street Station in London. It was the home of the Roman governor of Britain. The garden area was about 35m by 70m, within which was a series of pools, and a model of the palace can be seen on display in the Museum of London.

## Plants from Roman sites in Britain

The list of plants identified from Roman military, civilian, urban and rural sites in Britain has grown significantly in recent years.

The first long-term Roman residents were merchants and soldiers who were posted here. The soldiers were expected to be reasonably self-sufficient, although imported wine, olives and fish sauce augmented locally available produce. They grew some crops on military land, and, rather surprisingly opium poppies and cannabis were cultivated near Hadrian's Wall. Opium was used in cooking and for medicines, and the cannabis plant provided hemp for rope-making. Beer (*cervesa*) made from barley was popular with the troops, and it seems that the soldiers introduced carrots, cabbage, lentils and garlic to supplement their basic diet of bread (*panis militaris*), meat and cheese.

Some plants are obviously imported, such as dates and olives, but with others it is not so easy to be certain. Figs and grapes may have been grown in gardens, or even vineyards, as the climate was wetter and warmer in Britain during the Roman period, but it is probable that they were also imported in dried form. Planting vineyards in the Roman Empire was banned by the Emperor Domitian (AD 81–96), who was concerned that farmers were neglecting their grain crops in order to tend their vines. The edict was not reversed until AD 280 by the Emperor Probus, but it appears that the law was never rigorously enforced.

Archaeologists have excavated gardens in several Romano-British towns. Typical Roman courtyard gardens and open spaces probably used as gardens have been found, but plant evidence is sadly lacking at many of these urban sites. This is in part due to the fact that later buildings and gardening activities disturbed or destroyed any surviving plant material. However excavations in the early 20th century at Silchester (*Calleva Atrebatum*) near Reading proved to be very successful, largely because the town had been abandoned after the Roman period and lay undisturbed for centuries. Parsnips, celery, peas, corn-salad, carrots and radishes were among the plants grown at *Calleva*, the last four probably being cultivated Roman introductions. Some forms of onion (*allium*) and cabbage (*brassica*) were also grown but individual varieties are very hard to identify. It is likely that raspberries, strawberries and blackberries were picked in the wild, unless British

*A quince branch from a mosaic in Tunisia.*
*Photographer: Gilles Mermet*

*A rose incorporated in a first-century mosaic at Fishbourne Roman Palace.*

farmers were aware of Columella's advice to plant a bramble hedge by smearing a thick rope with ripe blackberries in autumn and bury it in a trench where a hedge was required. Remains of plants such as roses, mallows, violets, aquilegias and box were also found, so this suggests that citizens in *Calleva* planted formal or decorative gardens.

In towns where there has been continuous occupation since the Roman period, excavated Roman wells or water-logged sites have been some of the best sources of evidence. This is partly because the remains have lain undisturbed, but also because they survive longer in water-logged environments. Among the introduced Roman plants found at such sites in London are white mustard, lentils, flax, cucumber, coriander, fennel and dill. More unusual foods introduced by the Romans include alexanders, asparagus, purslane, apricots and peaches.

These cultivated plants were introduced mainly for their use as food. Bullaces, sweet and sour cherries, medlars, mulberries and quinces, as well as sweet chestnuts and walnuts found their way into Roman Britain, perhaps brought over in planting pots like those found at Pompeii and at Fishbourne Roman Palace. Pruning hooks suitable for fruit trees have been found at several sites, very similar to tools used today. One such pruning hook was found at Hartlip in Kent, and it is quite possible that the great orchards of Kent trace their origins back to the Roman period. At Colchester archaeologists found a particularly interesting selection of carbonised plant remains in a Roman shop, thanks to Boudicca's ruthless destruction of the town by fire in AD 61.

Anise, stone pine cones, gold-of-pleasure, flax, beans, lentils and coriander were identified, though it is not possible to say which were locally grown and which were imported.

All this suggests that the Roman occupation of Britain made a tremendous difference to the range of food available to their British hosts, although not everyone would have had access to all the newly available plants. Those in the south, living near towns or near a military establishment, would certainly have sampled a selection. Many wealthy and pro-Roman Britons copied Roman garden style in terms of design and planting, especially in the 3rd and 4th centuries AD. It is very likely that archaeologists in the future will learn a great deal more about Romano-British gardens, as interest in garden history grows and investigative techniques become ever more sophisticated.

# GARDENING TECHNIQUES

Much of the advice given to gardeners and farmers by Varro, Columella and others seems remarkably modern, and could be applied with good results today. In a way it is not surprising, as most people worked on the land, and tools and practices evolved to simplify labour-intensive jobs or to increase production. What is fortunate is that these techniques and developments were recorded by literate authors who had also had some practical experience. It is difficult to establish which of these techniques were used in Britain, although we can get some idea from iron tools discovered here. Soil composition sometimes indicates that the soil was improved with manure or better quality topsoil from elsewhere. Pliny writes that the Britons and Gauls knew about "feeding the earth with a kind of soil called marl", and chalk was also used as a soil improver. Where formal gardens have been established, as at Fishbourne, it is almost certain that foreign gardeners were employed. The local population would have had no experience or understanding of the requirements of a grand Roman garden, and must have regarded it with some amazement if not awe.

Columella in his book on agriculture gives a beginner's guide to setting up and running a garden. The fact that he writes it in the form of a poem does not mean that he does not give some very down-to-earth advice. He opens his manual by describing how to choose the best site:

> *"First for the varied garden let rich soil*
> *A place provide, which shows a crumbling glebe*
> *And loosened clods, and, dug, is like thin sand.*
> *Fit is the nature of the soil which grass*
> *Abundant grows and moistened brings to birth*
> *Elder's red berries...*
>
> *Let rivers flow adjacent to your plot,*
> *Whose streams the handy gardener may lead*
> *As aid to quench the garden's ceaseless thirst..."*

Columella next describes seasonal tasks, starting with autumn, when the soil should be turned and loosened with iron-shod spades, after rain. Then the soil should be further broken down with ploughs, mattocks and heavy rakes so the winter frosts can improve it. Winter is also the time to sharpen and mend tools.

In spring, he says that animal or human manure should be carried in baskets to the garden and liberally spread over it, and raked in. Then the gardener should mark divisions and make ridges in the beds with a hoe, and start sowing seed.

Pansies, violets, narcissi and marigolds were sown first, followed by herbs and vegetables. Once shoots appear the gardener must water and hoe the beds regularly. Some plants, such as radishes and basil, should be sown successively to provide a long harvesting season. Columella even gives advice on how to deal with pests and diseases. To prevent insect damage one could sprinkle plants with "unsalted lees of oil", or black soot, or drench them in horehound juice. If this does not work, Columella advises leading a young woman around the garden three times, and all the caterpillars in the trees will twist and tumble to earth. Mildew, clearly a serious problem, was blamed on the goddess Rubigo and to appease her it was recommended that a puppy should be sacrificed in her honour. This and other suggestions are macabre to say the least, and show that garden lore was an eccentric mixture of practical advice and magic.

Columella advises that most garden tasks should be completed by the end of August to allow the gardener to attend to the vines.

Vines were grown wherever the climate was suitable, so important were they for fruit, wine, decoration and for shade on pergolas. Varro recommended two ways of supporting them, the first being on a vertical post or a maple tree. The second method required a trellis of vertical and horizontal posts and was called the *compluvium* style. The uprights were to be made of oak or juniper, and could be reversed when the bottom ends rotted. The horizontal supports or yokes (*iuga*) were to be made of poles, reeds, cords or the vines themselves. They should be no higher than the height of a man.

Theophrastus wrote the first extensive botanical guide to plants, and also included advice for their cultivation. He wrote that, as a general rule, all vegetables and herbs need water and manure except rue. Water should be fresh and cold, and not from irrigation ditches, as these might contain weed seeds. Watering should be

*Harvesting grapes*
Photographer: Gilles Mermet

done early in the morning or the evening. Wilhelmina Jashemski discovered evidence of a useful watering method at Pompeii. The gardeners had placed "sombrero" shaped beds around trees which they used as soil troughs, so that water reached the roots more easily.

Theophrastus recommended a variety of sources for manure: wood ash, aviaries, humans, pigs, goats, sheep, and cows. Once collected, the gardener should mix it with straw. Lupins were used for green manuring, the growing plants being ploughed back into the soil to improve its balance of nutrients.

*Carrying manure out to the garden*

Theophrastus recommends transplanting of many perennials to raise taller stronger plants. Pliny writes that transplanted trees should be put into holes at least 60cm wide and deep. The holes should be lined with stones, broken pots or gravel, and smaller shrubs and trees should be at least a metre apart, the gap increasing with the eventual size of the mature plant.

Grafting trees appears to have been a widely used technique, and Columella lists four methods: cleft grafting (*insitio I*), bark grafting (*insitio II*), patch budding (*inoculata emplastratio*), and bore grafting (*terebratio*). Cato gives very detailed advice on the best method for pears or apples. The branch to be grafted was inserted into the parent tree between the bark and wood, and care was taken to angle it to ensure that water could not penetrate and rot it. Next it was smeared with a mixture of clay or chalk, cattle dung and a little sand, and split willow was wrapped around the grafted shoot to keep it in place and protect it. The graft and main tree were then wrapped in straw and bound tightly to prevent cold injuring them. Several different varieties could be grafted onto a tree at the same time.

New plants were also propagated by layering, a method recommended by Cato for blackberries, ivy, vines, figs, pomegranates, apples, and bay.

The layers could be grown in baskets or pots so that they could be transplanted more easily. Cuttings were made to produce new plants, myrtle and mulberries being two common examples. Collecting seed was a vital part of every gardener's job, and Theophrastus recommends collecting it early in the season, and not using it if it is more than four years old. Curiously he also says that when the gardener sows cumin, he should curse it furiously to ensure a good crop!

Specialist techniques were used to raise valued plants. The Emperor Tiberius supplied himself with cucumbers all year round by having them planted in wheeled trolleys. These were pushed out into the sunshine by day and wheeled inside at night to protect them from cold. Some gardeners poured warm water on to the roots of rose bushes to produce unnaturally early blooms.

Cato gives detailed advice on raising an asparagus bed which differs little from methods recommended today.

Remains of many of the tools mentioned in Latin texts have been found in Britain and differ very little from tools currently used. Iron spades were introduced to Britain by the Romans, and were ingeniously designed to use as little iron as possible while still producing an effective tool. The cutting edges of wooden spades were strengthened with an iron sheath, which could be rounded or square edged as required. A gardener would use a billhook for clearing scrub and lopping small branches. Although other Iron Age people used billhooks, the Roman design was superior and eventually replaced earlier types. The Roman army also introduced scythes for cutting grass, probably to provide hay for winter feed for animals. Pruning hooks were used for cutting leaves for fodder as well as pruning fruit and other trees and short bladed hoes were probably used for weeding. Rakes have also been found. They consist of wooden beams with series of iron prongs set into them, and were perhaps used for turning hay.

One tool yet to be discovered in Britain is the vinedresser's tool described by Columella. It developed from a billhook, and sounds rather similar to a

*Replica Roman garden tools*

Swiss Army knife, having several hooks shaped for performing a variety of tasks. These implements included two knives, a hook for hollowing out, a paring edge for smoothing out, a hatchet for chopping, and a spike for cutting in a narrow space. Although this is an extreme example of Roman ingenuity, double-headed or double purpose tools are not uncommon.

# List of Plants and Their Uses

The plants described below are a selection from approximately six hundred plants which Roman writers and modern archaeologists have recorded. Much of the information details medical applications, and there are some unusual remedies, which are not necessarily recommended.

The plants are listed alphabetically by their Latin name, followed by the common current English name or names.

 Native to Britain

 Pre-Roman introduction to Britain

 Roman introduction to Britain

 Roman (Italy and the Mediterranean)

 Culinary

 Utilitarian

 Ritual

 Medical

 Decorative

---

## Acanthus mollis / Bear's breeches

Pliny writes that there were two varieties of acanthus. One variety was *Acanthus mollis*, on which the Corinthian column capital is based according to Virgil. The second type was *Acanthus spinosus*. Both were used ornamentally in formal gardens to line paths, and they also had medical applications. The roots were used cooked and applied as a poultice to burns, sprains and gouty limbs. It was also recommended for preventing hair loss.

---

## Acorus calamus / Sweet flag

Sweet flag has been traded for 4000 years and according to Dioscorides, the best variety grew in India. As well as being used as a decorative plant, it was recommended to treat coughs if taken on its own, or mixed with terebinth resin (turpentine) "the smoke thereof being taken at the mouth through a funnel" (Dioscorides).

---

## Allium cepa / Onion

Onions were an important food to the Romans, and Dioscorides was familiar with white, red, round and long onions.. They were eaten raw, cooked, or preserved in salt. Pliny reckoned that because they made one's eyes water that they were good for dim vision. Mixed with salt and rue they were used to treat dog bites. Onion juice was mixed with chicken fat and rubbed on blisters and bunions to heal them, and also rubbed on balding heads as a hair restorative. Whether the patients treated in this way were banished from their families' presence is not recorded, but the smell must have been off-putting to say the least!

## Allium porrum / Leek

Originally cultivated in Egypt, two varieties were recognised by Columella and Martial, one being grown for its root, the other for its leaves. Pliny advises that nosebleeds can be cured by plugging the nostrils with chopped leek. Less controversially, he comments on its usefulness in curing coughs, catarrh and lung infections when pounded and mixed with barley water. Leeks also had a reputation as an aphrodisiac.

## Allium sativum / Garlic

Both purple and white forms of garlic were cultivated, and used in cooking and in salad dressings, and for several "country medicines" (Virgil). Pliny believed that the breath odour associated with eating garlic could be neutralised by eating roast beetroot afterwards. In earlier times it was used to treat madness, and was also taken with fresh coriander and wine as an aphrodisiac. One presumes that both partners drank this unappetising concoction!

## Allium schoenoprasum / Chives

Chives were apparently grown in a fort garden on Hadrian's Wall, as clumps can still be found growing wild there. Used both for cooking and in medicine, Pliny writes that the Emperor Nero ate only chives preserved in oil on certain fixed days of the month, to enhance his voice. Whether it made it louder or gave it more staying power, Pliny does not record.

## Althaea officinalis / Marshmallow

The word *altho* comes from the Greek word, meaning "to heal". Although marshmallow roots were used as food, the main use was as a poultice for wounds, bruises and tumours. It was crushed and boiled in wine which subsequently thickened and could be applied to the skin. The mixture could also be drunk for toothache. Pliny makes the unlikely observation that a marshmallow leaf placed on a scorpion paralyses it.

## ANAGALLIS ARVENSIS / SCARLET PIMPERNEL

Pliny writes that scarlet pimpernel flowers were eaten at Alexandria, and recommends them for a curious assortment of complaints: hypochondria, mange and freckles. *Anagallis* comes from the Greek word meaning "to laugh".

## ANCHUSA OFFICINALIS / ALKANET

Alkanet was used for dyeing wood and wax, and the root also thickened ointments for burns and ulcers. Fleas were killed when sprayed with a decoction of the roots in water.

## ANEMONE CORONARIA / ANEMONE

Anemones were used in chaplets (head garlands), and there were several cultivated species, red, purple and creamy white. The leaves resembled parsley, according to Pliny, and the plant was about 15cm high.

## ANETHUM GRAVEOLENS / DILL

Dill was one of the standard herbs supplied to every Roman fort, and has been found as far north as the Antonine Wall in Scotland. It was used to flavour food and, as a diuretic, was used to treat nursing mothers. Pliny says bluntly that it "causes belching".

## ANTHRISCUS CEREFOLIUM / CHERVIL

Chervil was eaten as a potherb, and its sharp and bitter flavour could be moderated by boiling it down and using it as a relish. An ancient "health food", it improved the condition of belly, stomach, kidneys and liver (Dioscorides). The seeds could be taken in vinegar to cure hiccups.

## ARBUTUS UNEDO / STRAWBERRY TREE

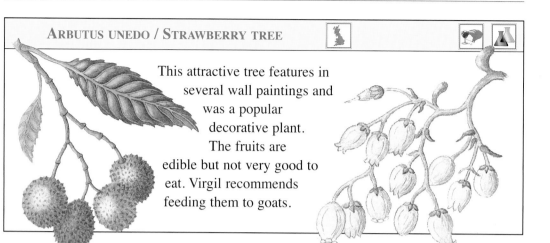

This attractive tree features in several wall paintings and was a popular decorative plant. The fruits are edible but not very good to eat. Virgil recommends feeding them to goats.

## ARTEMISIA ABROTANUM / SOUTHERNWOOD

The flowers of southernwood have a pleasant but heavy scent. Southernwood was valued for its magical properties and the protection it gave against malevolent spells. Drunk in wine it was an antidote for deadly poisons, and a spray of flowers under the pillow was said to act as a powerful aphrodisiac.

## ARTEMISIA ABSINTHIUM / WORMWOOD

Similar in properties to southernwood, wormwood was also used to flavour a wine called "absinthite". Leaves were strewn amongst clothes to repel moths and when the juice was mixed with ink it discouraged mice from eating papyrus scrolls. Legend has it that Roman soldiers planted wormwood along the roadside, so that they could put sprigs of it in their boots to ease their aching feet.

## ASPHODELUS RAMOSUS / ASPHODEL

Asphodel bulbs were roasted as food, and were considered a special delicacy when cut up and served with figs. Planted at the gate of a villa, asphodel was reputed to keep away the evil influence of sorcery.

## ATRIPLEX HORTENSIS / ORACHE

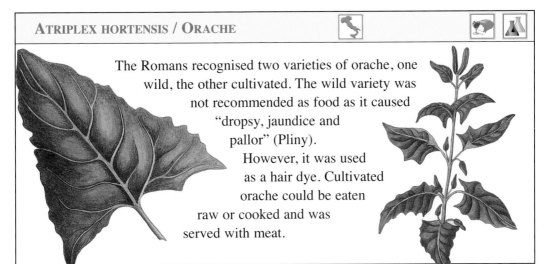

The Romans recognised two varieties of orache, one wild, the other cultivated. The wild variety was not recommended as food as it caused "dropsy, jaundice and pallor" (Pliny). However, it was used as a hair dye. Cultivated orache could be eaten raw or cooked and was served with meat.

## BETA VULGARIS / BEETROOT

Although it was a widely used potherb, Martial dismisses beetroots as "the insipid food of artisans". Sowings were made in spring or autumn, depending on the variety. One recipe for a salad mentioned by Pliny instructs the cook to mix cooked beetroot with lentils and beans. A decoction of liquid from wild beets was used for removing stains from clothes and parchment. These wild and cultivated beets were not the vivid purple colour of common varieties used today

## BORAGO OFFICINALIS / BORAGE

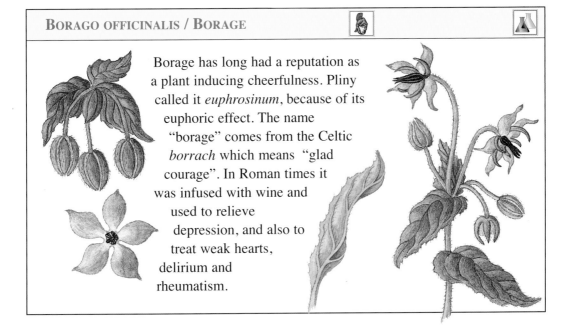

Borage has long had a reputation as a plant inducing cheerfulness. Pliny called it *euphrosinum*, because of its euphoric effect. The name "borage" comes from the Celtic *borrach* which means "glad courage". In Roman times it was infused with wine and used to relieve depression, and also to treat weak hearts, delirium and rheumatism.

## Brassica rapa / Turnip

Turnips were multi-purpose plants, which must have made them a popular inclusion in the vegetable garden. Both root and leaves were eaten. The juice of the leaves when mixed with mother's milk was used as an eye-wash. A cosmetic face-pack was made from mashed turnip, ground vetches, barley, wheat and lupins. In Britain hot mashed turnips could be put to good use as a cure for chilblains. Indeed turnips mashed with salt were recommended for all foot ailments. Pliny also says that a "wine" was made from them, though one doubts that it posed any serious competition to the more usual grape-based variety!

## Brassica sp. / the Cabbage family

Another multi-purpose family of plants, cabbages were an important food. Many types were cultivated, including floppy-leaved, curly-leaved, tight-hearted and open varieties. It was eaten raw to prevent drunkenness. It tasted best when lightly cooked (Dioscorides). Nitre or soda added to the cooking water maintained the bright green colour. Pliny's favourite variety was sprouts, but Apicius, a 1st century AD gourmet and cookery writer, despised them. Ashes of burnt cabbages, mixed with asafoetida and vinegar were applied as a depilatory, and the cooked mashed leaves were regarded as a comforting poultice for any inflammation. Cato extols the virtue of bathing young boys in urine collected from those on a diet of cabbages. He does not, however, record the reactions of the boys themselves to this treatment! Less controversially, Cato recommends scouring pots by boiling cabbage in them.

## Buxus sempervirens / Box

Gardeners used box extensively for clipped hedges in formal gardens, and carpenters regarded it as a first-rate carpentry wood because of its hardness and pale colour. Pliny observes that it does not float in water because of its denseness. Flutes were made from it, as well as boxes and other small items. Sprigs of box are often found in Roman coffins, in Britain as well as elsewhere, so it must have had some funerary significance.

## CALENDULA OFFICINALIS / MARIGOLD

Marigolds are among the earliest flowers in cultivation, and were used for decorations, and as a dye for fabrics, foods and cosmetics. An infusion was drunk to relieve sleeplessness and nervous tension.

## CANNABIS SATIVA / CANNABIS OR HEMP

Hemp was widely used for making strong twisted ropes and hunting nets. The seeds were crushed while green and used to treat earache, and the ripe seeds were eaten as a contraceptive. There is no record of the Romans having used the plant for its properties as a drug. However, a thousand years earlier the Scythians, who lived to the north of the Black Sea, threw cannabis plants onto hot stones to produce intoxicating fumes.

## CARUM CARVI / CARAWAY

Caraway root is edible and, when cooked, resembles parsnips. Julius Caesar refers to chara, a kind of bread made from caraway roots mixed with milk that was eaten by soldiers. The oil was used as a stimulant and a tonic. Dioscorides wrote that caraway was good for the stomach and chewing the seeds relieved indigestion and flatulence.

## CHENOPODIUM ALBUM / FAT HEN

The oily seeds and leaves of fat hen are edible and were a common food for poor people. Seeds of fat hen were found in the stomach of Tollund Man, who died in about 100 BC. The plant also yields a yellow dye.

## CHENOPODIUM BONUS-HENRICUS / GOOD KING HENRY

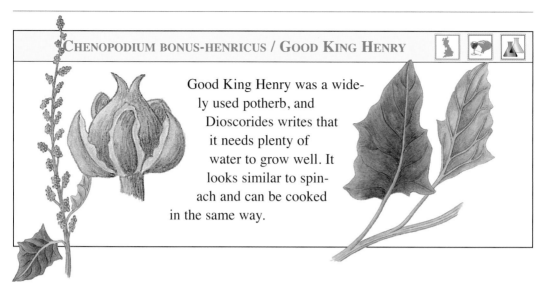

Good King Henry was a widely used potherb, and Dioscorides writes that it needs plenty of water to grow well. It looks similar to spinach and can be cooked in the same way.

## CICER ARIETINUM / CHICKPEA

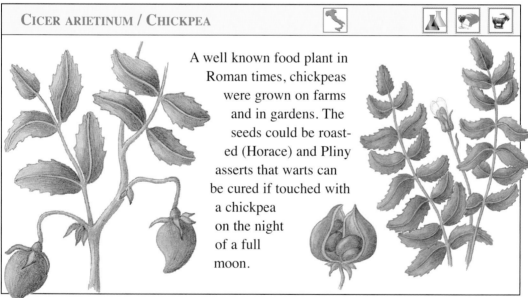

A well known food plant in Roman times, chickpeas were grown on farms and in gardens. The seeds could be roasted (Horace) and Pliny asserts that warts can be cured if touched with a chickpea on the night of a full moon.

## CICHORIUM ENDIVA , C. INTYBUS / ENDIVE, CHICORY

Both plants were grown in gardens and used for food. The juices could be used to treat fevers, when mixed with vinegar and oil of roses. A poultice made from either vegetable could be applied to treat both eye inflammations and heart trouble, depending on where it was placed.

## CITRON MEDICA / CITRON

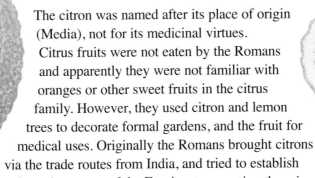

The citron was named after its place of origin (Media), not for its medicinal virtues.
Citrus fruits were not eaten by the Romans and apparently they were not familiar with oranges or other sweet fruits in the citrus family. However, they used citron and lemon trees to decorate formal gardens, and the fruit for medical uses. Originally the Romans brought citrons via the trade routes from India, and tried to establish them in various parts of the Empire, transporting them in the planter pots described earlier. Pliny comments that they would only grow in Media and Persia, but Roman gardeners proved otherwise. Several wall-paintings at Pompeii show citrons and lemons in flower and with fruits. The fruits and leaves were placed in clothes chests as a moth repellent, and the fruits were cooked with meat to help sweeten the breath. They probably tenderised the meat as well. Women swallowed the pips to counteract morning sickness, and fruits were dried and used to treat diarrhoea.

## CROCUS SATIVUS / SAFFRON CROCUS

Saffron crocuses were very valuable plants in Roman times for many reasons. The bulbs could be eaten, though Dioscorides says that they can be poisonous if taken in excess. Both red and yellow dyes could be obtained from the stamens and stigma. Powdered saffron was mixed with wine and sprayed in theatres to perfume them, and saffron oil was a common ingredient in perfumes and unguents. Reclining on a saffron pillow at a feast was supposed to prevent hangovers. Other "medical" uses were as an aphrodisiac and a cure for sleeplessness.

## CUCUMIS MELO / GOURD

Pliny wrote that gourds like to climb high and need supporting. The fruits could be moulded by constraining them in sheaves of plaited wicker. The stalk and green rind of the fruits were eaten, and remaining fruits were used as jugs in the bath-house, or even as jars for storing wine. Farmers dried gourds in smoke and stored their seeds in them.

## CUCUMIS SATIVUS / CUCUMBER

Cucumbers were grown on the ground or suspended on a frame. Romans in Italy preferred the small varieties, according to Pliny, whereas in the provinces larger ones were more popular. Cucumbers were long or round, and they came in a variety of colours. As well as being a popular food, raw or cooked with oil, vinegar and honey, cucumbers were used to treat several eye complaints. The seeds were pressed into lozenges and these were taken for dim vision, eye diseases and sore eyelids.

## CYDONIA OBLONGA / QUINCE

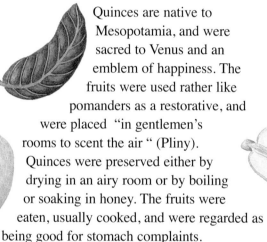

Quinces are native to Mesopotamia, and were sacred to Venus and an emblem of happiness. The fruits were used rather like pomanders as a restorative, and were placed "in gentlemen's rooms to scent the air " (Pliny). Quinces were preserved either by drying in an airy room or by boiling or soaking in honey. The fruits were eaten, usually cooked, and were regarded as being good for stomach complaints.

## CYNARA CARDUNCULUS / CARDOON

Cardoons are related to globe artichokes, and were used in much the same way, although the young stems were also eaten. The plants were grown commercially as well as in gardens, and the fields must have looked magnificent with the 2m high plants topped with large purple thistles. Pliny writes that the hearts were the most tender part, and that they were preserved in honey diluted with vinegar, and sometimes flavoured with cumin.

## ERUCA SATIVA / ROCKET

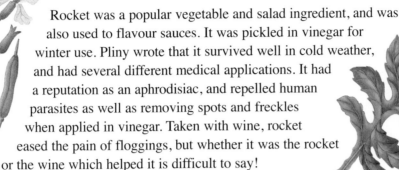

Rocket was a popular vegetable and salad ingredient, and was also used to flavour sauces. It was pickled in vinegar for winter use. Pliny wrote that it survived well in cold weather, and had several different medical applications. It had a reputation as an aphrodisiac, and repelled human parasites as well as removing spots and freckles when applied in vinegar. Taken with wine, rocket eased the pain of floggings, but whether it was the rocket or the wine which helped it is difficult to say!

## ERYSIMUM CHEIRI / WALLFLOWER

Wallflowers are probably the "yellow violets" mentioned in Roman literature. Apart from their use as decorative flowers, the roots mixed with vinegar and eaten quietened the spleen and soothed gout (Dioscorides).

## FAGUS SYLVATICA / BEECH

Virgil claimed that beech trees were the best shade trees, though plane trees were more commonly found in Pompeii. He also wrote that names cut into the bark grow with the tree, and the wood was good for firewood and for making drinking cups. Beech mast was fed to thrushes and dormice to fatten them up for the pot, and given to pigs, it livened them up and made the resulting pork light and digestible. Country people used thin branches and twigs to make baskets, and roof shingles were fashioned from the trunks.

## FICUS CARICA / FIG

Figs were brought to Britain, but possibly only in the dried form. Figs were sacred to Romulus and Remus, as the she-wolf reputedly suckled the twins under a fig tree. Pliny describes 29 cultivars, and comments on their medicinal usefulness: "Ripe figs are diuretic, laxative, sudorific and bring out pimples." Fig juice was used to curdle milk, like rennet, and was rubbed on meat to keep it fresh and to tenderise it. A "wine" and a syrup were made from figs, no doubt administered for much the same reasons as today.

## FOENICULUM VULGARE / FENNEL

Fennel is one of the oldest plants in cultivation, and legend has it that Prometheus carried down fire from heaven in its stem. It was regarded by the Romans as an early slimming aid, and its seeds were chewed to stave off hunger. Gladiators ate fennel to give them stamina and courage. The dried leaves were used to treat eye ailments, and snakes were reputed to suck the juice to improve their eyesight.

## GENISTA TINCTORIA / DYER'S GREENWEED

The yellow flowers were woven into chaplets, and the plant was often grown near beehives to attract bees to settle. The plant was also used to produce a yellow dye.

## GLADIOLUS COMMUNIS / GLADIOLUS

Apart from their decorative value, gladioli were used as food and as a tonic. Pliny wrote that the bulbs "make a pleasant food when boiled," and also improved the flavour and weight of bread. Bulbs were burnt and "smoke was inhaled every day through the mouth by some to increase briskness and greater strength" (Pliny). The crushed bulbs could also be applied as a liniment with oil, as a cure for chafings, abrasions and offensive armpits!

## GLYCYRRHIZA GLABRA / LIQUORICE

Pliny called it "the sweet root" and described it as a prickly plant with leaves. Liquorice juice was made into a drink. The thickened juice was placed under the tongue, to improve the voice, and swallowed to ease sore throats.

## HEDERA HELIX / IVY

Dioscorides mentions three varieties of ivy, white, black and helix. It was used extensively as a decorative plant, often growing over supports to produce "instant" topiary figures. It was known to harm walls of buildings and tombs. Ivy was sacred to Bacchus, and poets wore wreaths of a yellow-berried variety. Alexander the Great wore a wreath of ivy when he returned victorious from India and it was used generally for chaplets. Young ivy leaves were cooked in vinegar and eaten, but Dioscorides warns that eating too many berries causes sterility and madness. Ivy was used to produce a black hair dye, a contraceptive and a lice poison, so certainly counts as one of the more widely applied plants!

## HELICHRYSUM ITALICUM / GOLDFLOWER

Pliny describes goldflowers as "shining white" and the leaves as a "dull whitish colour like southernwood". Sprigs were placed in chests among clothes to protect them from insects. Romans valued the everlasting flowers, and fashioned chaplets from them to adorn statues of the gods. In the British Museum one can see a funeral wreath of goldflowers found in a Romano-Egyptian tomb.

## HELLEBORUS NIGER / CHRISTMAS ROSE

Probably planted in gardens from Roman times, hellebore seeds have been found in much earlier Neolithic burials. The poison was used to tip arrows, although Virgil comments on its bitter taste, so it appears the Romans took it internally despite its possibly fatal consequences.

## HUMULUS LUPULUS / HOPS

Hops were popular in Roman gardens and one of the few climbing plants used for decoration. Young hop leaves were sold as a vegetable in Roman markets in spring, to be eaten like asparagus.

## HYSSOPUS OFFICINALIS / HYSSOP

Dioscorides notes that there were two varieties of hyssop, one grown in gardens, the other found on mountains. It was used as an ingredient in medicines. Cooked with figs, water, honey and rue, it helped those suffering from chest problems, including asthma, coughs and catarrh. It was also prepared as a compress with figs and nitre for sprains and bruises. Bees found it attractive so it was often planted near hives. Its scent made it a valued ingredient in perfumes.

## ILEX AQUIFOLIUM / HOLLY

Holly was thought to have magical properties so was often planted in town and country gardens to ward off evil influences. Pythagoras claimed that a holly stick thrown at an animal to scare it would increase the length of the throw, such was its power. Crushed holly leaves mixed with salt were applied as a poultice for aching joints, and to help extract embedded objects.

## INULA HELENIUM / ELECAMPANE

Regarded as a cure-all by the Romans, elecampane was given its Latin name because Helen of Troy was reputedly gathering it when she was abducted by Paris. Thus a face-pack with elecampane juice was believed to give one a clear complexion and an attractive appearance. According to Pliny, Julia, the daughter of Emperor Augustus (27BC–AD14), ate candied elecampane roots to "help the digestion and increase mirth". The root of the plant is very bitter, but its juice is sweet. The root was dried and pounded into flour, and mixed with honey, raisins and dates to be taken as a tonic for a weak stomach. Perhaps not unconnected is the belief that the juice also expelled worms.

## IRIS SP. / IRIS

Several varieties of iris were known to the Romans, and it is not easy to distinguish between them from their descriptions. Dioscorides notes that irises came in many shades similar to a rainbow: white, pale blue, black, purple and azure. The roots were dried in the shade suspended from linen threads. The powdered root was used to treat coughs and sunburn, and in perfume manufacture. Pliny wrote that "red iris" roots were fastened to babies' clothing for them to chew when teething. The root was used externally for drawing out boils and whitlows, corns and warts. Apparently it was even more effective if it was gathered in the left hand and the name of the sufferer was said out loud!

## ISATIS TINCTORIA / WOAD

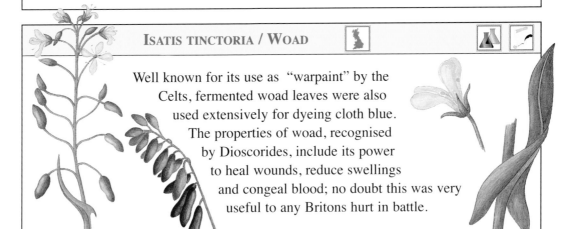

Well known for its use as "warpaint" by the Celts, fermented woad leaves were also used extensively for dyeing cloth blue. The properties of woad, recognised by Dioscorides, include its power to heal wounds, reduce swellings and congeal blood; no doubt this was very useful to any Britons hurt in battle.

## JUGLANS REGIA / WALNUT

Legend has it that when the gods lived on earth they dined on walnuts, hence their Latin name. Walnuts were thrown at weddings because they made such a clatter. The green rind was used as a hair dye, and shells were burnt and beaten with oil and wine to anoint babies' heads to make their hair grow more quickly. Cato writes that walnut trees create heavy shade, causing headaches to those who rest under them, and damage to plants growing nearby.

## JUNIPERUS COMMUNIS / JUNIPER

Virgil comments on juniper's fragrant wood, which was often used to make incense, and ancestral images were carved from it. The oily distillate was used to preserve books. Juniper juice mixed with oil was used to treat a rather alarming medical problem: "It doth kill wormes that are in the ears and doth quiet their noise and hissings" (Dioscorides).

## LACTUCA SATIVA / LETTUCE

Pliny knew many different sorts, green, purple, white, crinkly, narrow-leaved and broad-leaved, to name but a few. All lettuces were thought to be soporific. A round lettuce with a small root was called "eunuch's lettuce" as it checked men's amorous instincts. Lettuces were at their best in summer, but could be preserved in brine or honey and vinegar for the winter months. Leaves were applied to burns with salt before the blister formed.

## LAURUS NOBILIS / BAY

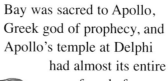

Bay was sacred to Apollo, Greek god of prophecy, and Apollo's temple at Delphi had almost its entire roof made from bay leaves. Bay was also placed on Jupiter's altar, and was regarded as a symbol of victory by the Romans, accompanying military dispatches, and decorating the spears and javelins of soldiers. It was also a symbol of peace, passed between enemies at the cessation of hostilities. Romans believed that bay was never struck by lightning, so the Emperor Tiberius wore a crown of it at all times. Doorways were decorated with it at New Year to bring good luck. Bay was used as an air freshener, and leaves were added to baths to relieve muscle pains and cramp. Cooks placed leaves under small cakes when they were baked.

## LAVANDULA DENTATA/ L. STOECHAS / LAVENDER

Lavender was valued for its aromatic and antiseptic properties. It derives its name from *lavare*, to wash, and the oil was added to bath water, an early aromatherapy treatment for headaches and faintness.

## LILIUM CANDIDUM / MADONNA LILY

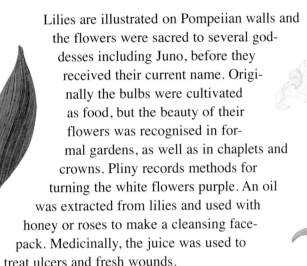

Lilies are illustrated on Pompeiian walls and the flowers were sacred to several goddesses including Juno, before they received their current name. Originally the bulbs were cultivated as food, but the beauty of their flowers was recognised in formal gardens, as well as in chaplets and crowns. Pliny records methods for turning the white flowers purple. An oil was extracted from lilies and used with honey or roses to make a cleansing face-pack. Medicinally, the juice was used to treat ulcers and fresh wounds.

## LINUM USITATISSIMUM / FLAX

Linen made from flax is one of the most ancient clothing fabrics, and the fibre was used to make fishermen's nets, napkins, theatre awnings and sails. Cleopatra reputedly had a purple linen sail on her boat when she went to meet Mark Antony at Actium. Thereafter, purple sails were used to distinguish the emperors' boats. Awnings of sky blue linen spangled with stars were stretched over Nero's amphitheatres, and on a more modest scale, white awnings were used in domestic *peristylia*. Cicero writes that documents and letters were sealed with linen threads. Linseed was used to make "a rustic porridge usually used for sacrifices" (Pliny).

## MALUS SP. / APPLES

Native crab apples have been used as food for thousands of years, but it seems likely that the Romans introduced the first cultivated varieties. Apples were commonly grafted onto quince or pear stock. Orchards may well have been planted in Britain as in Italy, and the fruits used as fresh or dried fruit, for cider-making and to treat diarrhoea and other stomach complaints.

## MELISSA OFFICINALIS / BALM

Balm was a favourite bee plant, the word *melissa* coming from the Greek word for honeybee. Hives were rubbed with balm and bees controlled with besoms made of its stalks. It was sacred to the goddess Diana. Leaves were mixed with wine to treat "griping of the bowels" (Pliny).

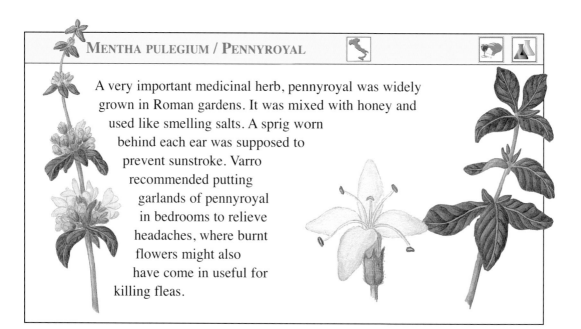

## MENTHA PULEGIUM / PENNYROYAL

A very important medicinal herb, pennyroyal was widely grown in Roman gardens. It was mixed with honey and used like smelling salts. A sprig worn behind each ear was supposed to prevent sunstroke. Varro recommended putting garlands of pennyroyal in bedrooms to relieve headaches, where burnt flowers might also have come in useful for killing fleas.

## MENTHA SP. / MINT

In Greek mythology Minthe was a nymph loved by Pluto. Pluto's jealous wife transformed the unlucky creature into a plant. Mint was used to flavour wine and sauces and was regarded as good for the stomach. A paste of mint and honey was taken to sweeten the breath. Ovid describes mint as the herb of hospitality. Romans scoured banqueting tables with it, scattered it on the floor, and even stuffed cushions with it to perfume the air. Brides wore garlands of mint on their wedding day.

## MESPILUS GERMANICA / MEDLAR

Pliny writes that there were three varieties of medlar, and all had a wide spreading habit. A "wine" was made from the fruit, which were also eaten. A medlar seed was found during excavations at Silchester.

## MORUS NIGRA / MULBERRY

Mulberries were introduced to Rome from India in about 160BC. The colour of the fruit was said to come from Pyramus, who killed himself under a mulberry tree, according to Ovid. Pliny disliked the flavour of the fruit but says that a mouthwash was made out of it. A hair dye was made from the fruit by soaking them in black fig leaves, wine and rainwater. Since the wood is pliable, theatre seats and hoops for garlands were made from it. A little honey mixed with cooked mulberries eased tonsillitis (Dioscorides).

## MYRRHIS ODORATA / SWEET CICELY

Dioscorides wrote that sweet cicely grows on marshy ground, and also in gardens in Egypt. A mouthwash was made from the plant to treat toothache.

## MYRTUS COMMUNIS / MYRTLE

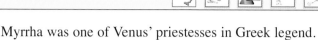

Myrrha was one of Venus' priestesses in Greek legend. Venus transformed her into a tree to protect her from too ardent a suitor. The flowers were often woven into bridal wreaths. Myrtle was used in purification rites before battle, and also by soldiers after a bloodless victory. Two sacred myrtles grew in Romulus' temple in Rome, one the "patricians" myrtle, the other the "plebians" myrtle. The fortunes of each group of citizens were said to wax and wane according to the health of the respective trees. It was grown in gardens and parks for its decorative virtues, its scent and its useful berries. Before peppercorns were available, myrtle berries were used instead and chewing a few berries sweetened the breath. A non-alcoholic drink was made from them, and the crushed berries made a darkening hair dye. Black myrtle was the best variety for medicinal use. The leaves were simmered in oil and water and laid in oil in sunshine. They could then be used to treat ulcers and other skin problems.

## NEPETA CATARIA / CATMINT

Burning catmint drove away snakes, as they disliked the smoke and smell (Pliny). Catmint was placed underneath the bedclothes of those who feared being bitten in the night.

## NIGELLA SATIVA / BLACK CUMIN

Black cumin was grown as a food by the ancient Egyptians, and may be the "fitches" mentioned in Isaiah, valued for its seeds. Romans sprinkled them on bread, and like juniper, used them to spice food before peppercorns were imported. The seeds could also be mixed with vinegar and applied to treat corns (Dioscorides).

## OCIMUM BASILICUM / BASIL

In ancient Greece, basil symbolised hatred and misfortune. Dioscorides warned that eating too much basil would dull the sight and cause sneezing, but on the plus side it helped ease flatulence! Pliny thoroughly disapproved of basil as a foodstuff, writing that overindulgence caused madness, coma, and breeding of worms, scorpions and lice. However, he did approve of some uses for it. Mixed with cobbler's blacking, basil removed warts. Farmers had a use for it too. They fed it to horses and asses at the appropriate time as an equine and asinine aphrodisiac.

## OLEA EUROPEA / OLIVE

According to Pliny, olives were introduced to Rome in 581 BC, and their cultivation spread rapidly. Olives were crushed and sweetened with brine, and with bread and cheese, constituted the main diet of the poor. The third pressing produced poor quality oil that was used in lamps. Round amphorae from Spain containing olive oil were imported in large quantities to Britain.

## ORIGANUM SP. / MARJORAM, OREGANO

The name oregano comes from the Greek *oros-ganos*, meaning "joy of the mountain". Oregano was used in cooking, but was also an important garland and strewing herb, because of its strong pleasant perfume. It also repelled snakes and other poisonous beasts. One variety, dittany from Crete, had special virtues according to Dioscorides. He wrote that it helped remove splinters and thorns from feet, and goats who had eaten it spontaneously expelled any arrows inadvertently embedded in them!

## PAEONIA OFFICINALIS / PEONY

 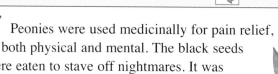

Peonies were used medicinally for pain relief, both physical and mental. The black seeds were eaten to stave off nightmares. It was believed that they had magic powers, and Dioscorides gives very precise instructions for getting the maximum protection from them. The flowers should be "picked in the heat of the dog days, and hung about the neck, against poisonings, bewitchings, fears, devils and fevers."

## PAPAVER SOMNIFERUM / OPIUM POPPY

Known as a powerful soporific in Roman times, at least two varieties of poppy were also cultivated and used as food. The white seeds were roasted and served as a second dinner course with honey. Seeds were also sprinkled on top of loaves glazed with egg. Tarquinius the Proud symbolically knocked the heads off the tallest poppies in his garden in response to his son's apparently unreasonable requests, sent via his envoys. One imagines that they beat a hasty retreat after such a warning.

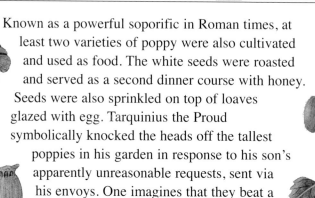

## PASTINACA SATIVA / PARSNIP

Parsnips were one of Emperor Tiberius' favourite vegetables, and he requisitioned a personal supply annually from Germany. The root was cooked with honey and was recommended as delicious and good for the stomach by Dioscorides.

## PETROSELINUM CRISPUM / PARSLEY

Parsley was a very popular herb especially in sauces, and at least three cultivated varieties were known. Fish benefitted from it too, as parsley was added to ponds with ailing fish to revive them. Parsley was dedicated at funeral feasts to the memory of the dead.

## PHYSALIS ALKEKENGI / BLADDER CHERRY

Bladder cherries are an ancient decorative garden plant, grown in Rome and described by Dioscorides.

## PIMPINELLA ANISUM / ANISEED

Aniseed was widely cultivated during the Roman period and earlier. It was used to flavour sauces, and put under the bottom crusts of bread. Because it prevented indigestion, according to Virgil, small meal cakes containing aniseed were often served after heavy meals, especially wedding feasts. Sprigs of aniseed were hung over pillows to reduce insomnia.

## PORTULACA OLERACEA / PURSLANE

A fresh tasting salad plant, purslane soothes and heals toothache and sore gums. Pliny mentions two rather unexpected virtues of eating it. Firstly, it checks lust and amorous dreams, and secondly, if one rubs one's head with it one will not suffer from catarrh for a whole year.

## PRUNUS ARMENIACA / APRICOT

A native of China, apricots were introduced to the Romans via the ancient silk routes. Columella called the apricot tree *armenium*.

## PRUNUS CERASUS / SOUR CHERRY

Pliny wrote that cherries came from Pontus in the 1st century BC, and they reached Britain about a hundred years later. Red and black varieties were known and the fruit were eaten straight off the tree or dried and stored like olives in casks. Virgil commented that cherries were grafted on plum stock, possibly to reduce the height of the mature tree.

## PRUNUS DOMESTICA / PLUM, DAMSON

Pliny writes that there was a wide variety of plums from which to choose. Ovid's plums were yellow, while those described by Virgil sound like bullaces (*P.institia*). Martial and Columella describe a fruit like a damson (*P. damascena*). The fruits were eaten fresh or dried, and when boiled in wine the leaves soothed tonsils, sore gums and throats.

## PRUNIS DULCIS / ALMOND

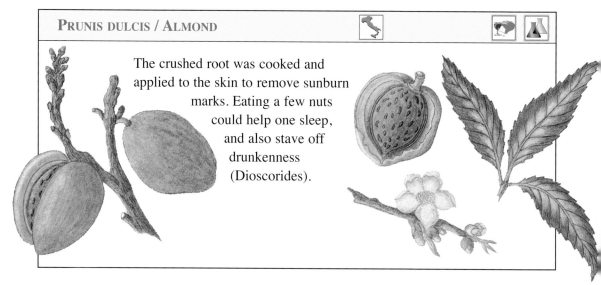

The crushed root was cooked and applied to the skin to remove sunburn marks. Eating a few nuts could help one sleep, and also stave off drunkenness (Dioscorides).

## PUNICA GRANATUM / POMEGRANATE

Pomegranates were associated with the legend of Persephone, and figure widely in Roman mosaics and wall paintings. Pliny knew nine varieties, and wrote that they were used in many medicines. Pomegranates were the classical symbol of fertility, and were eaten especially by childless women. The flowers were used as an amulet against eye troubles and burnt pomegranate rind repelled gnats. The rind was also used for dressing leather, and dyeing cloth. Pomegranates were stored after hardening in sea water for three days, and drying in the sun for another three days. They were kept in large jars of sand (Varro).

## PYRUS COMMUNIS / PEAR

Pliny described raw pears as "indigestible", but cooked "remarkably wholesome and pleasant". Falernian pears were made into a type of perry, and other varieties into a jam-like conserve, with apples and quinces.

## RAPHANUS SATIVUS / RADISH

Dioscorides recommended them as food with the caveat that they caused "belching and wind". Pliny took exception to these unfortunate side effects and relegated the radish to "a vulgar sort of diet". He did however recommend using oil of radishes for polishing ivory.

## ROSA SP. / ROSE

Roses were probably the most popular decorative plant in Roman times, and Cleopatra is reputed to have seduced Mark Antony while he was knee-deep in rose petals. Roman banquets were garlanded with roses, sometimes to an excessive degree. The Emperor Domitian ensured a winter supply by having them sent from Egypt. The scent was highly valued and attar of roses was a staple ingredient in perfumes. It was even used to scent drinks and the soles of one's feet. Its medical applications included treating eye infections. Pliny preferred propagation by grafting, as sowing seeds was too slow a method, and pruning was recommended to improve the plants. Roses were commercially grown around Campania, and on market days the streets were red with thousands of garlands for sale.

## ROSMARINUS OFFICINALIS / ROSEMARY

Rosemary was plaited into crowns and garlands, and rosemary boiled in water was recommended by Dioscorides to warm one up before taking exercise.

## RUBIA TINCTORUM / MADDER

Madder was a very important dye plant for producing shades of red and orange to colour wool and leather. It grew wild but was also planted in fields and under olive trees.

### RUBUS FRUTICOSUS, R. IDAEUS / BLACKBERRY, RASPBERRY

Blackberries were used as a deterrent hedging plant and to make medicines to treat sore mouths and inflammation of the bowel. Raspberries grew all over Britain and were mentioned in a Mediterranean context by the Roman poet Propertius (c.50–16 BC).

### RUMEX ACETOSA, R. CRISPUS / SORREL, DOCK

Pliny preferred the wild varieties to those grown in gardens, and recommended eating them with pearl barley. The juice made an effective mouthwash and chewing the roots strengthened loose teeth. Dock has been identified as Pliny's *herba britannica*, which is credited with having cured Julius Caesar's soldiers of scurvy.

### RUTA GRAVEOLENS / RUE

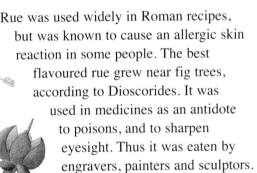 

Rue was used widely in Roman recipes, but was known to cause an allergic skin reaction in some people. The best flavoured rue grew near fig trees, according to Dioscorides. It was used in medicines as an antidote to poisons, and to sharpen eyesight. Thus it was eaten by engravers, painters and sculptors.

### SALIX SP. / WILLOW

Willow was used extensively in gardens and by farmers. Using pollarding techniques, an acre of willow provided enough supports for 25 acres of vineyard. Strips of willow bark were used as withies, and the shoots for ties. Osiers were plaited into baskets and "luxurious easy chairs" (Pliny). Dioscorides recommended the bark for pain relief and low fever. It was effective because the bark contains salicylic acid, the basic ingredient in aspirin.

Virgil wrote that practice shields were made from willow, and Theophrastus added that this was because willow was "self-repairing", i.e. it closed up over any cuts.

## SALVIA OFFICINALIS / SAGE

The name comes from *salvere*, "to save" and sage was used to staunch wounds and clean ulcers. It was a sacred plant to be gathered with some ceremony. It was never cut with an iron blade as iron salts react with the chemicals in sage, a fact known to the Romans. Sage was also used as a hair dye.

## SAMBUCUS NIGRA / ELDER

"Sambucus" comes from the Greek word *sambuke* meaning a musical pipe, and Pliny wrote that country people made horns or trumpets from its hollow branches. Elderberries were boiled and eaten, and the juice used as a hair dye.

## SAPONARIA OFFICINALIS / SOAPWORT

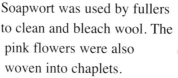

Soapwort was used by fullers to clean and bleach wool. The pink flowers were also woven into chaplets.

## SCILLA BIFOLIA / SCILLA

Scillas were grown extensively in Gaul and used to produce a deep red dye. Pliny gave complicated instructions for preserving the bulbs to use for making oil, vinegar and wine.

## SEMPERVIVUM TECTORUM / HOUSELEEK

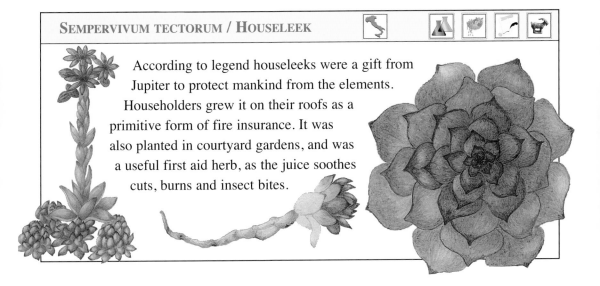

According to legend houseleeks were a gift from Jupiter to protect mankind from the elements. Householders grew it on their roofs as a primitive form of fire insurance. It was also planted in courtyard gardens, and was a useful first aid herb, as the juice soothes cuts, burns and insect bites.

## SINAPIS ALBA / WHITE MUSTARD

Widely used for food, the value of white mustard was such that Emperor Diocletian fixed its price in his edict of 301 AD. It was also burnt in braziers as a fumigant.

## SMYRNIUM OLUSTRATUM / ALEXANDERS

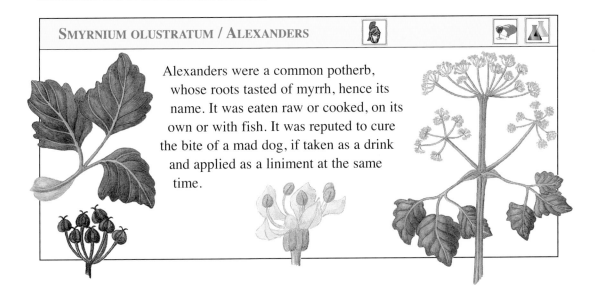

Alexanders were a common potherb, whose roots tasted of myrrh, hence its name. It was eaten raw or cooked, on its own or with fish. It was reputed to cure the bite of a mad dog, if taken as a drink and applied as a liniment at the same time.

## TAXUS BACCATA / YEW

Despite the fact that we now regard yew as a useful tree for hedges and topiary, the Romans did not use it, partly because it was poisonous. Pliny wrote that it had "a gloomy terrifying appearance". However, the wood was used for furniture ornamentation and for making bows.

## THYMUS SP. / THYME

Many different varieties of thyme were known to the Greeks and Romans and the plant had both internal and external applications. Oil of thyme was used in bath-houses for massage, and Roman soldiers added it to their baths to give them vigour. Dioscorides writes that a mild potion was made from thyme, for those who "are squeamish and bad-stomached and unsavoury belchers". Pliny recommended thyme as an antidote for snake bites. Virgil and other authors describe its importance as a bee plant.

## TILIA SP. / LIME

Lime trees were useful shade providers in gardens, and the wood was pliable enough to make ribbons, chaplet bands, and baskets. Pliny wrote that it was particularly useful because it was "worm-proof".

## TRIGONELLA FOENO-GRAECUM / FENUGREEK

Fenugreek was grown as a potherb, and a flour could be made from it for treating inflammations. Cream of fenugreek was used as a shampoo.

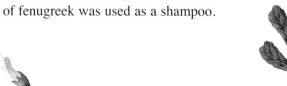

## ULMUS CAMPESTRIS / ELM

Elms were widely used as living vine supports in vineyards, planted in rows. They also provided shade in gardens. New leaves were cooked in sauces, and older leaves, bark and branches were crushed and moistened to make a poultice to treat skin diseases and wounds.

## URTICA DIOICA / STINGING NETTLES

Despite Pliny's comment "What can be more hateful than the nettle?", in Roman times nettles were considered very useful. The young leaves provided food "for the frugal" (Horace) and weavers used the fibrous stems to make cloth. We get our word "net" from nettles. The dried root was used as a depilatory and as an antidote for a range of poisons including hemlock. Roman soldiers are credited with introducing a particularly vicious form (*U. pilulifera*) to use as a local anaesthetic, and as a flail to keep themselves warm in our chillier climate.

## VALERIANA OFFICINALIS / VALERIAN

The name "valerian" comes from the Latin verb *valere*, "to be in good health". It has a strong scent and was used in unguents. Sprinkled between bedclothes it induced sleep, and pounded with lily petals and dried it was used as an ancient form of dusting powder.

## VERBASCUM THAPSUS / MULLEIN

According to legend, mullein was given to Ulysses to protect him from the sorcery of Circe, who changed the rest of his crew into pigs. The tall stems of mullein were dipped into tallow and used as tapers, especially at funeral processions.

## VERBENA OFFICINALIS / VERVAIN

Vervain has been a sacred plant in many ancient cultures, despite its uninteresting appearance. In Roman culture vervain was sacred to Venus and so love potions were made from it. It decorated altars and temples, and it was believed to bring good luck.

Ambassadors wishing to make peace (*verbeniari*) ritually carried vervain as a symbol of their intentions.

## VICIA FABA / BEAN

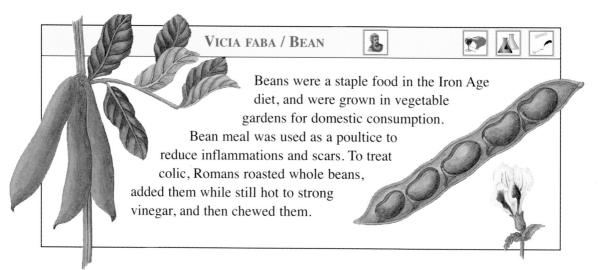

Beans were a staple food in the Iron Age diet, and were grown in vegetable gardens for domestic consumption.

Bean meal was used as a poultice to reduce inflammations and scars. To treat colic, Romans roasted whole beans, added them while still hot to strong vinegar, and then chewed them.

## VINCA MINOR / PERIWINKLE

Periwinkle was used as a decorative ground cover on banks in gardens where other plants would not grow. It was admired as a wreath and garland plant because of its pliable stems and charming flowers. The word "vinca" comes from *vincire*, meaning "to bind".

## VIOLA ODORATA / SWEET VIOLET

Another plant dedicated to Venus, violets were one of the most important decorative flowers for gardens, chaplets, wreaths and garlands. They were often used at banquets partly for their attractiveness and partly because the scent was reputed to lessen the effects of overindulgence. One type of wine was even flavoured with violets.

Purple violets, crushed and taken in water, were used to treat epilepsy in children. A commercial nursery sector developed in response to demand for increasing quantities of violets and the poet Horace grumbled that the Romans spent more time raising violets than they spent on growing olives. A word of warning here: it is not always clear if the viola in Roman writing is indeed viola odorata, as the name "violet" was used to include wallflowers and stocks as well.

## VITIS VINIFERA / VINE

There is a large quantity of contemporary information about raising vines which testifies to their importance in Roman life. Many varieties were known, used for eating and wine-making. Domestic wine production was a standard activity for country dwellers, and there were also large commercially-run vineyards to provide city dwellers, soldiers and connoisseurs with a range of everyday and expensive wines. Wines imbibed by the Romans came from Greece, Cyprus, North Africa and Turkey, the last having a reputation for causing headaches.

In gardens, vines were often multi-purpose plants, providing grapes for the table and wine-making, and shade for pergolas and walkways. Different vine preparations were used medicinally, and fresh white grapes were given to those recovering from illness.

Several Roman vineyards have been located in Britain.

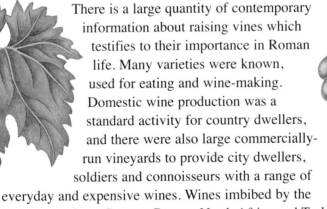

# PLANT INDEX

## A SELECTION OF PLANTS USED DURING THE ROMAN PERIOD

| | | | |
|---|---|---|---|
| Achillea | *Achillea sp.* | *Acanthus spinosus/mollis* | Bear's breeches |
| Ageratum | *Achillea viscosa* | *Acer sylvestris* | Maple |
| Alder | *Alnus glutinosa* | *Achillea millefolium* | Yarrow |
| Alexanders | *Smyrnium olustratrum* | *Achillea ptarmica* | Sneezewort |
| Alkanet | *Anchusa officinalis* | *Achillea sp.* | Achillea |
| Almond | *Prunus dulcis* | *Achillea viscosa* | Ageratum |
| Aloe | *Aloe vulgaris* | *Acinos arvensis* | Basil thyme |
| Alyssum | *Alyssum sp.* | *Acorus calamus* | Sweet flag |
| Anemone | *Anemone coronaria* | *Arctium lappa* | Greater burdock |
| Angelica | *Angelica sylvestris* | *Aegopodium podograria* | Ground-elder |
| Aniseed | *Pimpinella anisum* | *Agrostemma githago* | Corncockle |
| Apple | *Malus sp.* | *Ajuga reptans* | Bugle |
| Apricot | *Prunus armeniaca* | *Alcea sp.* | Hollyhock |
| Argemone | *Thalictrum flavum* | *Alchemilla vulgaris* | Lady's mantle |
| Arum | *Arum maculatum* | *Alisma plantago-aquatica* | Water plantain |
| Ash | *Fraxinus excelsior* | *Allium cepa* | Onion |
| Asphodel | *Asphodelus albus* | *Allium dioscorides* | Garden moly |
| Autumn crocus | *Colchicum autumnale* | *Allium porrum* | Leek |
| Bachelors buttons | *Pyrethrum parthenium* | *Allium sativum* | Garlic |
| Balm | *Melissa officinalis* | *Allium schoenoprasum* | Chives |
| Balsam (Touch-me-not) | *Impatiens noli-tangere* | *Alnus glutinosa* | Alder |
| Barren strawberry | *Potentilla sterilis* | *Aloe vulgaris* | Aloe |
| Basil | *Ocimum basilicum* | *Althaea officinalis* | Marshmallow |
| Basil thyme | *Acinos arvensis* | *Alyssum sp.* | Alyssum |
| Bay | *Laurus nobilis* | *Anagallis arvensis* | Scarlet pimpernel |
| Bean | *Vicia faba* | *Anagallis coerula* | Blue pimpernel |
| Bear's breeches | *Acanthus spinosus/mollis* | *Anchusa officinalis* | Alkanet |
| Beech | *Fagus sylvatica* | *Anemone coronaria* | Anemone |
| Beet | *Beta vulgaris* | *Anemone silvestris* | Windflower |
| Bell flowers | *Campanula* | *Anethum graveolens* | Dill |
| Betony | *Betonica officinalis* | *Angelica sylvestris* | Angelica |
| Bindweed | *Convolvulus arvensis* | *Anthriscus cerefolium* | Chervil |
| Birch | *Betula sp.* | *Antirrhinum majus* | Snapdragon |
| Birds' foot trefoil | *Lotus corniculatus* | *Apium graveolens* | Celery |
| Black cumin | *Nigella sativa* | *Aquilegia vulgaris* | Columbine |
| Black mustard(black) | *Sinapis nigra* | *Arbutus unedo* | Strawberry tree |
| Black nightshade | *Solanum nigrum* | *Armeria maritima* | Thrift |
| Blackberry | *Rubus fruticosus* | *Artemisia abrotanum* | Southernwood |
| Bladder cherry | *Physalis alkekengi* | *Artemisia absinthium* | Wormwood |
| Blue pimpernel | *Anagallis coerula* | *Artemisia vulgaris* | Mugwort |
| Bog myrtle | *Myrica gale* | *Arum dioscorides* | Cuckoopint |
| Borage | *Borago officinalis* | *Arum maculatum* | Edderwort |
| Box | *Buxus sempervirens* | *Arum maculatum* | Arum |
| Bryony | *Brionia dioica* | *Asphodelus albus* | Asphodel |
| Buckthorn | *Rhamnus alaternus* | *Aster amellus* | Michaelmas daisy |
| Bugle | *Ajuga reptans* | *Atractylis gummifera* | Pinethistle |
| Bullace | *Prunus institia* | *Atriplex hortensis* | Orache |
| Bulrush | *Cyperus rotundus* | *Atropa bella-donna* | Deadly nightshade |
| Butcher's broom | *Ruscus aculeatus* | *Beta vulgaris* | Beet |
| Buttercup | *Ranunculus sp.* | *Betonica officinalis* | Betony |
| | | *Betula sp.* | Birch |

| | | | |
|---|---|---|---|
| Cabbage | *Brassica sp.* | *Borago officinalis* | Borage |
| Calamint | *Calamintha ascendens* | *Brassica nigra* | Black mustard |
| Campion | *Silene vulgaris* | *Brassica rapa* | Turnip |
| Campion (red) | *Silene dioica* | *Brassica sp.* | Cabbage |
| Campion (white) | *Silene latifolia* | *Brionia dioica* | Bryony |
| Cannabis/hemp | *Cannabis sativa* | *Buxus sempervirens* | Box |
| Caper | *Capparis spinosa* | *Calamintha ascendens* | Calamint |
| Caraway | *Carum carvi* | *Calendula officinalis* | Marigold |
| Cardamom | *Elettaria cardamomum* | *Calluna vulgaris* | Heather |
| Cardoon | *Cynara cardunculus* | *Camelina sativa* | Gold-of-Pleasure |
| Catmint | *Nepeta cataria* | *Campanula latifolia* | Throatwort |
| Celery | *Apium graveolens* | *Campanula* | Bell flower |
| Chervil | *Anthriscus cerefolium* | *Campanula rotundifolia* | Harebell |
| Chickpea | *Cicer arietinum* | *Cannabis sativa* | Cannnabis/hemp |
| Chicory | *Cichorium intybus* | *Capparis spinosa* | Caper |
| Chives | *Allium schoenoprasum* | *Carduus sp.* | Thistle |
| Christmas rose | *Helleborus niger* | *Carpinus betulus* | Hornbeam |
| Cinquefoil | *Potentilla reptans* | *Carum carvi* | Caraway |
| Cistus | *Cistus salvifolius* | *Centaurea cyanus* | Cornflower |
| Citron | *Citrus medica* | *Cerinthe major* | Honeywort |
| Coltsfoot | *Tussilago farfara* | *Chelidonium maius* | Greater celandine |
| Columbine | *Aquilegia vulgaris* | *Chenopodium album* | Fat hen |
| Comfrey | *Symphytum officinale* | *Chenopodium bonus-henricus* | Good King Henry |
| Common fleabane | *Pulicaria vulgaria* | *Chenopodium vulvaria* | Goosefoot |
| Coriander | *Coriandrum sativum* | *Chrysanthemum coronarium* | Crown daisy |
| Corn marigold | *Chrysanthemum segetum* | *Chrysanthemum segetum* | Corn marigold |
| Corn salad | *Valerianella locusta* | *Cicer arietinum* | Chickpea |
| Corncockle | *Agrostemma githago* | *Cichorium endivia* | Endive |
| Cornelian cherry | *Cornus mas* | *Cichorium intybus* | Chicory |
| Cornflower | *Centaurea cyanus* | *Cistus salvifolius* | Cistus |
| Cowslip | *Primula veris* | *Citrus medica* | Citron |
| Cranberry | *Vaccinium oxycoccos* | *Clematis alba* | Old mans beard |
| Cranesbill family | *Geranium sp.* | *Colchicum autumnale* | Autumn crocus |
| Crown daisy | *Chrysanthemum coronarium* | *Conium maculatum* | Hemlock |
| Cuckoopint | *Arum dioscorides* | *Conopodium majus* | Pignut |
| Cucumber | *Cucumis sativus* | *Convallaria majalis* | Lily of the valley |
| Cumin | *Cuminum cyminum* | *Convolvulus arvensis* | Bindweed |
| Cyclamen | *Cyclamen hederifolium* | *Coriandrum sativum* | Coriander |
| Cyclamen (Greek) | *Cyclamen graecum* | *Cornus mas* | Cornelian cherry |
| Cypress | *Cupressus sempervirens* | *Cornus mascula* | Dogwood |
| Dames violet | *Hesperis matronalis* | *Crataegus sp.* | Hawthorn |
| Damson | *Prunus damascena* | *Crithmum maritimum* | Rock samphire |
| Dandelion | *Taraxacum sp.* | *Crocus sativus* | Saffron crocus |
| Daphne | *Daphne gonidium* | *Cucumis melo* | Melon |
| Deadly nightshade | *Atropa bella-donna* | *Cucumis sativus* | Cucumber |
| Delphinium | *Delphinium peregrinum* | *Cuminum cyminum* | Cumin |
| Devil's-bit scabious | *Succisa pratensis* | *Cupressus sempervirens* | Cypress |
| Dill | *Anethum graveolens* | *Cuscuta europaea* | Dodder |
| Dittany | *Origanum dictamnus* | *Cyclamen graecum* | Cyclamen (Greek) |
| Dock | *Rumex crispus* | *Cyclamen hederifolium* | Cyclamen |
| Dodder | *Cuscuta europaea* | *Cydonia oblonga* | Quince |
| Dogwood | *Cornus mascula* | *Cynara cardunculus* | Cardoon |
| Dyers greenweed | *Genista tinctoria* | *Cynoglossum officinale* | Hound's tongue |
| Edderwort | *Arum maculatum* | *Cyperus rotundus* | Bulrush |
| Elder | *Sambucus nigra* | *Daphne gonidium* | Daphne |
| | | *Datura stramonium* | Thornapple |

| | | | |
|---|---|---|---|
| Elecampane | *Inula helenium* | *Delphinium consolida* | Larkspur |
| Elm | *Ulmus campestris* | *Delphinium peregrinum* | Delphinium |
| Endive | *Cichorium endivia* | *Dianthus sp.* | Pink |
| Fat hen | *Chenopodium album* | *Digitalis purpurea* | Foxglove |
| Fennel | *Foeniculum vulgare* | *Dipsacus fullonum* | Teasel |
| Fenugreek | *Trigonella foena-graecum* | *Doronicum pardaliariches* | Leopard's bane |
| Field penny-cress | *Thlapsi arvensi* | *Echinops ritro* | Globethistle |
| Fig | *Ficus carica* | *Elettaria cardamomum* | Cardamom |
| Flax | *Linum usitatissimum* | *Eruca sativa* | Rocket |
| Fleabane var. | *Inula candida* | *Erysimum cheiri* | Wallflower |
| Forget-me-not | *Myosotis sp.* | *Euphorbia sp.* | Spurge |
| Foxglove | *Digitalis purpurea* | *Fagus sylvatica* | Beech |
| Fumitory | *Fumaria parvifolia* | *Ferula tingitana* | Silphium |
| Galeopsis | *Scrophularia peregrine* | *Ficus carica* | Fig |
| Garden moly | *Allium dioscorides* | *Filipendula ulmaria* | Meadowsweet |
| Garlic | *Allium sativum* | *Foeniculum vulgare* | Fennel |
| Gentian | *Gentiana lutea* | *Fragaria vesca* | Strawberry |
| Germander | *Teucrium* | *Fraxinus excelsior* | Ash |
| Ginger | *Zingiber officinale* | *Fraxinus ornus* | Manna ash |
| Gladiolus | *Gladiolus communis* | *Fumaria parvifolia* | Fumitory |
| Globeflower | *Trollius europaeus* | *Galanthus nivalis* | Snowdrop |
| Globethistle | *Echinops ritro* | *Galega officinalis* | Goat rue |
| Goat rue | *Galega officinalis* | *Galium verum* | Lady's bedstraw |
| Gold-of-Pleasure | *Camelina sativa* | *Genista tinctoria* | Dyers greenweed |
| Golden thistle | *Scolymus hispanicus* | *Gentiana lutea* | Gentian |
| Goldflower | *Helichrysum italicum* | *Geranium sp.* | Cranesbill family |
| Good King Henry | *Chenopodium bonus-henricus* | *Gladiolus communis* | Gladiolus |
| Goosefoot | *Chenopodium vulvaria* | *Glycyrrhiza glabra* | Liquorice |
| Gorse | *Ulex europaeus* | *Hedera helix* | Ivy |
| Greater burdock | *Arctium lappa* | *Helianthemum sp.* | Rock rose |
| Greater celandine | *Chelidonium maius* | *Helichrysum italicum* | Goldflower |
| Ground Elder | *Aegopodium podograria* | *Heliotropium europaeum* | Heliotrope |
| Guelder rose | *Viburnum opulus* | *Helleborus niger* | Christmas rose |
| Harebell | *Campanula rotundifolia* | *Hesperis matronalis* | Dame's violet |
| Harts tongue | *Scolopendrium vulgare* | *Humulus lupulus* | Hops |
| Hawthorn | *Crataegus sp.* | *Hyoscyamus niger* | Henbane |
| Heather | *Calluna vulgaris* | *Hypericum crispum* | Hypericum |
| Heliotrope | *Heliotropium europaeum* | *Hypericum apollinis* | St John's wort |
| Hemlock | *Conium maculatum* | *Hyssopus officinalis* | Hyssop |
| Henbane | *Hyoscyamus niger* | *Ilex aquifolium* | Holly |
| Henna | *Lawsonia alba* | *Impatiens noli-tangere* | Balsam (Touch-me-not) |
| Holly | *Ilex aquifolium* | *Inula candida* | Fleabane var. |
| Hollyhock | *Alcea sp.* | *Inula helenium* | Elecampane |
| Holm-oak | *Quercus ilex* | *Iris sp.* | Iris |
| Honeysuckle | *Lonicera periclymenum* | *Isatis tinctoria* | Woad |
| Honeywort | *Cerinthe major* | *Jasminum fruticans* | Jasmine(wild) |
| Hops | *Humulus lupulus* | *Juglans regia* | Walnut |
| Horehound | *Marrubium vulgare* | *Juniperus communis* | Juniper |
| Hornbeam | *Carpinus betulus* | *Lactuca sativa* | Lettuce |
| Hound's tongue | *Cynoglossum officinale* | *Lapsana communis* | Nipplewort |
| Houseleek | *Sempervivum tectorum* | *Lathyrus aphaca* | Yellow pea |
| Hypericum | *Hypericum crispum* | *Laurus nobilis* | Bay |
| Hyssop | *Hyssopus officinalis* | *Lavandula sp.* | Lavender |
| Iris | *Iris sp.* | *Lawsonia alba* | Henna |
| Ivy | *Hedera helix* | *Lens culinaris* | Lentil |
| | | *Lepidium campestre* | Pepperwort |

| | | | |
|---|---|---|---|
| Jasmine(wild) | Jasminum fruticans | Lepidium sativum | Pennycress |
| Jujube | Zizyphus vulgaris | Leucanthemum vulgare | Ox-eye daisy |
| Juniper | Juniperus communis | Levisticum officinale | Lovage |
| Lady's bedstraw | Galium verum | Lilium candidum | Madonna lily |
| Lady's mantle | Alchemilla vulgaris | Lilium chalcedonicum | Lily |
| Larkspur | Delphinium consolida | Lilium martagon | Martagon lily |
| Lavender | Lavandula sp. | Linaria vulgaris | Toadflax |
| Leek | Allium porrum | Linum usitatissimum | Flax |
| Lentil | Lens culinaris | Lithospermum officinale | Lithospermum |
| Leopard's Bone | Doronicum Caucasicum | Lonicera periclymenum | Honeysuckle |
| Lesser celandine | Ranunculus ficaria | Lotus corniculatus | Birds' foot trefoil |
| Lettuce | Lactuca sativa | Lupinus sp. | Lupin |
| Lily | Lilium chalcedonicum | Lychnis coronaria | Rose campion |
| Lily of the valley | Convallaria majalis | Lychnis flos-cuculi | Ragged robin |
| Lime | Tilia sp. | Malus sp. | Apple |
| Liquorice | Glycyrrhiza glabra | Malva sp. | Mallow |
| Lithospermum | Lithospermum officinale | Mandragora officinarum | Mandrake |
| Lovage | Levisticum officinale | Marrubium vulgare | Horehound |
| Lucerne | Medicago sativa | Matthiola incana | Stock |
| Lupin | Lupinus sp. | Medicago sativa | Lucerne |
| Madder | Rubia tinctoria | Melilotus officinalis | Sweet clover/melilot |
| Madonna lily | Lilium candidum | Melilotus officinalis | Melilot |
| Mallow | Malva sp. | Melissa officinalis | Balm |
| Mandrake | Mandragora officinarum | Mentha aquatica | Water mint |
| Manna ash | Fraxinus ornus | Mentha pulegium | Pennyroyal |
| Maple | Acer sylvestris | Mentha sp. | Mint |
| Marigold | Calendula officinalis | Mentha spicata | Spearmint |
| Marshmallow | Althaea officinalis | Mespilus germanica | Medlar |
| Martagon lily | Lilium martagon | Morus nigra | Mulberry |
| Meadowsweet | Filipendula ulmaria | Myosotis sp. | Forget-me-not |
| Medlar | Mespilus germanica | Myrica gale | Bog myrtle |
| Melilot | Melilotus officinalis | Myrrhis odorata | Sweet Cicely |
| Melon | Cucumis melo | Myrtus communis | Myrtle |
| Michaelmas daisy | Aster amellus | Narcissus sp. | Narcissus |
| Mint | Mentha sp. | Nepeta cataria | Catmint |
| Mistletoe | Viscum album | Nerium oleander | Oleander |
| Mugwort | Artemisia vulgaris | Nigella sativa | Black cumin |
| Mulberry | Morus nigra | Nymphaea alba | Waterlily |
| Mullein | Verbascum thapsus | Ocimum basilicum | Basil |
| Myrtle | Myrtus communis | Olea europea | Olive |
| Narcissus | Narcissus sp. | Onobrychis vicifolia | Sainfoin |
| Nipplewort | Lapsana communis | Origanum dictamnus | Dittany |
| Old mans beard | Clematis alba | Origanum sp. | Oregano/Marjoram |
| Oleander | Nerium oleander | Paeonia officinalis | Peony |
| Olive | Olea europea | Pancratium maritimum | Sea-daffodil |
| Onion | Allium cepa | Papaver rhoeas | Poppy |
| Opium poppy | Papaver somniferum | Papaver somniferum | Opium poppy |
| Orache | Atriplex hortensis | Parietaria judaica | Pellitory |
| Oregano/Marjoram | Origanum sp. | Pastinaca sativa | Parsnip |
| Ox-eye daisy | Leucanthemum vulgare | Petroselinum crispum | Parsley |
| Parsley | Petroselinum crispum | Physalis alkekengi | Bladder cherry |
| Parsnip | Pastinaca sativa | Pimpinella anisum | Aniseed |
| Pasque flower | Pulsatilla vulgaris | Pinus | Pine |
| Pea | Pisum sativum | Pinus pinea | Stone pine |
| Peach | Prunus persica | Piper nigrum | Pepper |
| | | Pistacia lentiscus | Pistachio |

| | | | |
|---|---|---|---|
| Pear | *Pyrus communis* | *Pisum sativum* | Pea |
| Pellitory | *Parietaria judaica* | *Plantago major* | Plantain |
| Pennycress | *Lepidium sativum* | *Platanus orientalis* | Plane |
| Pennyroyal | *Mentha pulegium* | *Polygonum maculosa* | Redshank |
| Peony | *Paeonia officinalis* | *Populus sp.* | Poplar |
| Pepper | *Piper nigrum* | *Portulaca oleracea* | Purslane |
| Pepperwort | *Lepidium campestre* | *Potentilla anserina* | Silverweed |
| Periwinkle | *Vinca minor* | *Potentilla reptans* | Cinquefoil |
| Pignut | *Conopodium majus* | *Potentilla sterilis* | Barren strawberry |
| Pine | *Pinus* | *Primula veris* | Cowslip |
| Pinethistle | *Atractylis gummifera* | *Primula vulgaris* | Primrose |
| Pink | *Dianthus sp.* | *Prunella vulgaris* | Self-heal |
| Pistachio | *Pistacia lentiscus* | *Prunus armeniaca* | Apricot |
| Plane | *Platanus orientalis* | *Prunus cerasus* | Sour cherry |
| Plantain | *Plantago major* | *Prunus damascena* | Damson |
| Plum | *Prunus domestica* | *Prunus domestica* | Plum |
| Pomegranate | *Punica granatum* | *Prunus dulcis* | Almond |
| Poplar | *Populus sp.* | *Prunus institia* | Bullace |
| Poppy | *Papaver rhoeas* | *Prunus lusitanica* | Portugal laurel |
| Portugal laurel | *Prunus lusitanica* | *Prunus persica* | Peach |
| Primrose | *Primula vulgaris* | *Prunus spinosa* | Sloe |
| Purslane | *Portulaca oleracea* | *Pulicaria vulgaria* | Common fleabane |
| Quince | *Cydonia oblonga* | *Pulsatilla vulgaris* | Pasque flower |
| Radish | *Raphanus sativus* | *Punica granatum* | Pomegranate |
| Ragged robin | *Lychnis flos-cuculi* | *Pyrethrum parthenium* | Bachelors buttons |
| Ragwort | *Senecio cineraria* | *Pyrus communis* | Pear |
| Raspberry | *Rubus idaeus* | *Quercus ilex* | Holm-oak |
| Redshank | *Polygonum maculosa* | *Ranunculus ficaria* | Lesser celandine |
| Rhubarb | *Rheum rhaponticum* | *Ranunculus sp.* | Buttercup |
| Rock rose | *Helianthemum sp.* | *Raphanus sativus* | Radish |
| Rock samphire | *Crithmum maritimum* | *Reseda luteola* | Weld |
| Rocket | *Eruca sativa* | *Rhamnus alaternus* | Buckthorn |
| Rose | *Rosa sp.* | *Rheum rhaponticum* | Rhubarb |
| Rose campion | *Lychnis coronaria* | *Rhus coriara* | Sumach |
| Rosemary | *Rosmarinus officinalis* | *Rosa sp.* | Rose |
| Rue | *Ruta graveolens* | *Rosmarinus officinalis* | Rosemary |
| Saffron crocus | *Crocus sativus* | *Rubia tinctorum* | Madder |
| Sage | *Salvia sp.* | *Rubus fruticosus* | Blackberry |
| Sainfoin | *Onobrychis vicifolia* | *Rubus idaeus* | Raspberry |
| Salad burnet | *Sanguisorba minor* | *Rumex acetosa* | Sorrel |
| Salsify | *Tragopogon porrifolius* | *Rumex crispus* | Dock |
| Scabious | *Scabiosa columbaria* | *Ruscus aculeatus* | Butcher's broom |
| Scarlet pimpernel | *Anagallis arvensis* | *Ruta graveolens* | Rue |
| Sea squill | *Urginea maritima* | *Salix sp.* | Willow |
| Sea-daffodil | *Pancratium maritimum* | *Salvia sp.* | Sage |
| Self-heal | *Prunella vulgaris* | *Sanguisorba minor* | Salad burnet |
| Service tree | *Sorbus domestica* | *Sambucus nigra* | Elder |
| Silphium | *Ferula tingitana* | *Saponaria officinalis* | Soapwort |
| Silverweed | *Potentilla anserina* | *Satureja hortensis* | Summer savory |
| Sloe | *Prunus spinosa* | *Satureja montana* | Winter savory |
| Smilax | *Smilax aspera* | *Scabiosa columbaria* | Scabious |
| Snapdragon | *Antirrhinum majus* | *Scilla bifolia* | Squill |
| Sneezewort | *Achillea ptarmica* | *Scilla maritima* | Sea squill |
| Snowdrop | *Galanthus nivalis* | *Scolopendrium vulgare* | Harts tongue |
| Soapwort | *Saponaria officinalis* | *Scolymus hispanicus* | Golden thistle |
| | | *Scrophularia peregrine* | Galeopsis |

| | | | |
|---|---|---|---|
| Sorrel | *Rumex acetosa* | *Sedum sp.* | Stonecrop |
| Sour cherry | *Prunus cerasus* | *Sempervivum tectorum* | Houseleek |
| Southernwood | *Artemisia abrotanum* | *Senecio cineraria* | Ragwort |
| Sow thistle | *Sonchus arvensis* | *Silene latifolia* | Campion (white) |
| Spearmint | *Mentha spicata* | *Silene dioica* | Campion (red) |
| Speedwell | *Veronica officinalis* | *Silene vulgaris* | Campion |
| Spurge | *Euphorbia sp.* | *Sinapis alba* | White mustard |
| Squill | *Scilla bifolia* | *Smilax aspera* | Smilax |
| St John's wort | *Hypericum apollinis* | *Smyrnium olustratrum* | Alexanders |
| Stinging nettle | *Urtica dioica* | *Solanum nigrum* | Black nightshade |
| Stitchwort | *Stellaria graminea* | *Sonchus arvensis* | Sow thistle |
| Stock | *Matthiola incana* | *Sorbus domestica* | Service tree |
| Stone pine | *Pinus pinea* | *Stachys* | Wound wort |
| Stonecrop | *Sedum sp.* | *Stellaria graminea* | Stitchwort |
| Strawberry | *Fragaria vesca* | *Succisa pratensis* | Devils-bit scabious |
| Strawberry tree | *Arbutus unedo* | *Sweet violet* | Viola odorata |
| Sumach | *Rhus coriara* | *Symphytum officinale* | Comfrey |
| Summer savory | *Satureja hortensis* | *Tamarix gallica* | Tamarisk |
| Sweet Cicely | *Myrrhis odorata* | *Taraxacum sp.* | Dandelion |
| Sweet clover/melilot | *Melilotus officinalis* | *Taxus baccata* | Yew |
| Sweet flag | *Acorus calamus* | *Teucrium sp.* | Germander |
| Sweet violet | *Viola odorata* | *Thalictrum flavum* | Argemone |
| Tamarisk | *Tamarix gallica* | *Thlapsi arvensi* | Field penny-cress |
| Teasel | *Dipsacus fullonum* | *Thymus sp.* | Thyme |
| Thistle | *Carduus sp.* | *Tilia sp.* | Lime |
| Thornapple | *Datura stramonium* | *Tragopogon porrifolius* | Salsify |
| Thrift | *Armeria maritima* | *Trigonella foenum-graecum* | Fenugreek |
| Throatwort | *Campanula latifolia* | *Trollius europaeus* | Globeflower |
| Thyme | *Thymus sp.* | *Tuber cibanum* | Truffle |
| Toadflax | *Linaria vulgaris* | *Tussilago farfara* | Coltsfoot |
| Truffle | *Tuber cibanum* | *Ulex europaeus* | Gorse |
| Turnip | *Brassica rapa* | *Ulmus campestris* | Elm |
| Valerian | *Valeriana officinalis* | *Urginea maritima* | Sea squill |
| Vervain | *Verbena officinalis* | *Urtica dioica* | Stinging nettle |
| Vetch | *Vicia sativa* | *Vaccinium oxycoccos* | Cranberry |
| Vine | *Vitis vinifera* | *Valeriana officinalis* | Valerian |
| Wallflower | *Erysimum cheiri* | *Valerianella locusta* | Corn salad |
| Walnut | *Juglans regia* | *Veratrum album* | White false hellebore |
| Water mint | *Mentha aquatica* | *Verbascum thapsus* | Mullein |
| Waterlily | *Nymphaea alba* | *Verbena officinalis* | Vervain |
| Waterplantain | *Alisma plantago-aquatica* | *Veronica officinalis* | Speedwell |
| Wayfaring tree | *Viburnum lantana* | *Viburnum lantana* | Wayfaring tree |
| Weld | *Reseda luteola* | *Viburnum opulus* | Guelder rose |
| White false hellebore | *Veratrum album* | *Vicia faba* | Bean |
| White mustard | *Sinapis alba* | *Vicia sativa* | Vetch |
| Willow | *Salix sp.* | *Vinca minor* | Periwinkle |
| Windflower | *Anemone silvestris* | *Viola odorata* | Sweet violet |
| Winter savory | *Satureja montana* | *Viscum album* | Mistletoe |
| Woad | *Isatis tinctoria* | *Vitis vinifera* | Vine |
| Wormwood | *Artemisia absinthium* | *Zingiber officinale* | Ginger |
| Wound Wort | *Stachys* | *Ziziphus vulgaris* | Jujube |
| Yarrow | *Achillea millefolium* | | |
| Yellow pea | *Lathyrus aphaca* | | |
| Yew | *Taxus baccata* | | |

# MEANINGS OF SELECTED LATIN NAMES FOR PLANTS

| | | | | |
|---|---|---|---|---|
| *abrotanum* | southernwood | | *minor* | lesser |
| *absinthium* | wormwood | | *melo* | black, or fruit tree. |
| *album* | white | | *mollis* | soft |
| *anisum* | uneven (from Greek) | | *montana* | growing on mountains |
| *arvensis* | pertaining to farmland | | *niger* | black |
| *baccata* | berrylike | | *nobilis* | noble, renowned |
| *basilicum* | royal | | *oblonga* | oblong |
| *candidum* | shining white | | *odorata* | fragrant |
| *cardunculum* | thistle-like | | *officinalis* | useful, used in medicine |
| *carica* | sedge | | *oleracea* | pertaining to gardens |
| *cerasus* | cherry | | *peregrinum* | foreign |
| *cereifolium* | waxy-leaved | | *pratensis* | grown in meadows |
| *communis* | common, universal | | *pulegium* | pennyroyal |
| *coronaria* | suitable for a garland | | *ramosu* | branching |
| *crispum* | curly | | *regia* | royal |
| *dentata* | toothed | | *sativum* | cultivated |
| *domestica* | for household use | | *sempervirens* | evergreen |
| *faba* | bean | | *siculum* | Sicilian |
| *fruticosus* | bushy | | *somniferum* | narcotic |
| *germanica* | German | | *sylvaticus* | wood |
| *glabra* | smooth | | *Thapsus* | a town in Africa |
| *graveolens* | strong smelling | | *tinctoria* | dyeing |
| *helenium* | of Helen (of Troy) | | *usitatissimum* | usual, customary |
| *helix* | spiral, twisted | | *vinifera* | wine making |
| *hortensis* | pertaining to gardens | | *vulgaris* | ordinary |
| *maior* | greater | | | |

# BIBLIOGRAPHY

**The following papers from "Garden Archaeology"**

Council for British Archaeology Research Report 78 ed. A.E. Brown   1991

| | |
|---|---|
| Murphy, P. and Scaife R. (3) | The environmental archaeology of gardens |
| Bond, C.J. and Iles, R. | Early gardens in Avon and Somerset |
| Zeepvat, R. | Roman gardens in Britain |
| Davies, R.W. | The Roman Military Diet, *Britannia II (1971)* |
| Williams, D. | Viticulture in Roman Britain, *Britannia VIII (1977)* |
| Van der Veen, M., Livarda, A., Hill, A. | New Plant Foods in Roman Britain *Environmental Archaeology 2008, vol 13, no 1* |
| Boon, G.C. | Silchester: The Roman City of Calleva *David and Charles   1974 (rev.)* |
| Bown, Deni | RHS Encyclopedia of Herbs and their uses *Dorling Kindersley   1995* |
| Ciarallo, Annamaria | Gardens of Pompeii *L'Erma di Bretschneider      2000* |
| Cunliffe, B.W. | Excavations at Fishbourne, Vol I Society of Antiquaries  1971 |
| Cunliffe, B.W. (4) | In "Ancient Roman Gardens » *Dumbarton Oaks, Washington DC, USA 1981* |
| Cunliffe, B.W. Down, A.G. Rudkin, D.J. | Chichester Excavations 9: Excavations at Fishbourne 1969-1988 *Chichester District Council   1996* |
| Farrar, Linda | Gardens of Italy and the Western Provinces of the Roman Empire *Council for British Archaeology 1996* |
| Godwin, Sir Harry | The History of the British Flora *CUP 1975* |
| Grimal, Pierre | Les Jardins Romains   *Paris  1969* |
| Jashemski, W. | The Gardens of Pompeii, Herculaneum and the Villas destroyed by Vesuvius *New Rochelle 1979* |
| Jashemski, W. | Roman Gardens in Tunisia *The American Journal of Archaeology 1995* |
| Manning, W.H. | Catalogue of Romano-British Iron Tools, Fittings and Weapons in the British Museum *BMP 1985* |
| Roach, F.A. | The Cultivated Fruits of Britain *Blackwell 1985* |
| Stearn, W.T. | Botanical Latin *David and Charles 3rd edn. 1983* |
| White, K.D. | Greek and Roman Technology *Thames and Hudson 1984* |
| White, K.D. | Roman Farming *Cornell University Press, Ithaca, New York 1970* |

**Latin and Greek literature**

| | |
|---|---|
| Apicius ( 1st century AD) | De Re Coquinaria |
| Cato | De Re Rustica |
| Columella | De Re Rustica |
| Dioscorides | The Greek Herbal of Dioscorides |
| Horace | Odes |
| Pliny the Elder | Historia Naturalis |
| Pliny the Younger | Letters and Panegyrics I and II |
| Theophrastus | Enquiry into Plants I and II |
| Varro | De Re Rustica |
| Virgil | The Georgics |

# Sussex Archaeological Society

The Sussex Archaeological Society is one of the oldest such organisations in the world and in addition to opening historic properties and museums to the public, is active in the fields of archaeological and historical research in the county.

Members of the Society (with the exception of Associates) receive three issues of the Sussex Past and Present newsletter a year and the annual volume, Sussex Archaeological Collections, an illustrated collection of essays and reports. The publications contain articles covering both history and archaeology in Sussex and news from the properties.

There is an interesting and varied programme of walks, digs, visits and conference and all members are entitled to free entry to the Society's library, museums and properties. The library, situated in Barbican House at Lewes, has an extensive range of Sussex material and is open throughout the year, including weekends, except at Christmas. Members also receive half-price entry to selected English Heritage properties in Sussex and Hampshire.

A full-time professional research officer is on hand to help members with their own projects and is also responsible for the Society's own activities throughout the county.

For further details please contact the Membership Secretary, Sussex Archaeological Society, Barbican House, 169 High Street, Lewes, Sussex, BN7 1YE. Tel: 01243 789829.